DATE DUE

Town House

This book is also available in a German language edition.
(ISBN 978-3-7643-8609-2)

Graphic Design and Drawings: Sebastian Schaal, Martin Trefon

Translation from German: Julian Reisenberger, Weimar

Library of Congress Control Number: 2008936173

Bibliographic information published by the German National Library
The German National Library lists this publication in the Deutsche Nationalbibliografie;
detailed bibliographic data are available on the Internet at http://dnb.ddb.de

© 2009 Birkhäuser Verlag AG
Basel · Boston · Berlin
P.O.Box 133, CH-4010 Basel, Switzerland
Part of Springer Science+Business Media

Printed on acid-free paper produced from chlorine-free pulp. TCF ∞

Printed in Germany

ISBN 978-3-7643- 8610-8

9 8 7 6 5 4 3 2 1   www.birkhauser.ch

Günter Pfeifer and Per Brauneck

Town Houses

A Housing Typology

Birkhäuser
Basel · Boston · Berlin

Contents

Preface

The city as we know it today does not fulfil the demands we will place on it in the future. In view of ongoing transformations in society and changing patterns of work, we need to develop a model of the city that is able to anticipate such developments while simultaneously taking into account the existing building fabric. We need to rethink planning methods and goals with a view to fostering a "vibrant mixture" in our cities.

The town house has an important role to play in this. Our perception of urban apartments is often negative: we associate them with communal staircases with long, dark corridors in cramped and anonymous apartment blocks. The most desirable residential form is, by contrast, a detached family house rather than a town house. In the age of globalisation, however, it seems that a change is gradually coming about. Greater energy efficiency is more easily achieved through collective approaches. The anonymity within the community offers potential for new, unconventional ways of living. The variety of cultural activities available, the close proximities and manifold recreational possibilities that metropolitan cities offer have made them attractive again. Today, the density of urban environments is no longer regarded as constrictive but as a potential and a quality.

City centres are experiencing a renaissance as desirable places to live in. Existing residential housing, however, only rarely fulfils contemporary demands. The old patterns of flats with two, three or four rooms, a kitchen and bathroom are being converted, extended or replaced. A shift in the typology of the town house is taking place, but only gradually. Opportunities for realising new buildings or redensification using fundamentally new building types, and therefore the chance to interpret and accommodate current tendencies, arise only sporadically. This volume focuses on the kinds of adaptable and dynamic structures that are evident in these building types.

As with the first two volumes in this series on housing typologies, this book also originated out of research conducted at the Department of Architecture at the University of Darmstadt. The focus of our research is a holistic consideration of housing with a view to developing a prospective typology catalogue for the design of residential buildings. Together with our students, new building types have been developed that take current as well as future developments into consideration. These building types are shown alongside built examples from experienced architects. The selection of projects – while not exhaustive – aims to illustrate sustainable tendencies in the development of typologies.

In the first two volumes of this series, on courtyard houses and row houses, we have presented housing typologies that can be extended on a minimum of two sides, often three sides, and can therefore be combined to form relatively dense urban structures. The town house types shown in this volume stand in the same tradition, which will also be continued in the fourth volume on single houses.

The town house typologies are shown at a scale of 1:500 and are presented in a uniform manner to enable the reader to compare the individual projects. The small scale is a factor of the large size of many of the projects. Typical floor plans in some examples have been coloured to make complex building structures easier to discern and are denoted in shades of grey in the individual storeys. Furnishings are represented abstractly in keeping with the small scale and to aid legibility. The projects are illustrated by floor plans with sections or isometric drawings where appropriate. In most cases only a typical floor plan is shown to explain the basic system of the internal structure. Economic advantages resulting from particular typological arrangements of floor plans are noted in the accompanying description.

The variety of town house typologies are organised in different categories: row, twin row, single-aspect row, continuous and perforated perimeter block and infill. Here we have consciously chosen to differentiate between different volumetric constellations rather than different access typologies. On the one hand, access typologies are becoming increasingly hybrid, compound and accordingly difficult to categorise. On the other, a typological classification according to urban situation allows planners and architects to use the examples as concrete sources of inspiration for analogue situations. Similarly, the spectrum of different typological solutions shown in this volume is also intended to motivate the designer to push forward the boundaries of conventional standards and explore new directions.

Living in the city

"Down with character!" proclaims Rem Koolhaas in his text "The Generic City" and proceeds to describe the impact and advantages of global uniformity: "The great originality of the generic city is simply to abandon … what has outlived its use." In the metropolitan cities of the modern world the boundaries between public and private have shifted; the need to form transitions and thresholds is no longer evident. The real changes in the city as well as the shift in our perception of the city are readily apparent and Koolhaas' assertion that *civitas* as an expression of the public realm and community is a thing of the past, is justified.

The anonymity of the city is increasingly regarded as a quality. Freedom from interpersonal or family obligations allows one to pursue leisure activities more intensively and promises a more direct and vital experience of life. The quality of "public space", a term previously used dogmatically as the backbone of post-modern urban design, is currently disintegrating; in its place a new kind of urban environment is arising that is characterised by anonymity and a higher density of cultural activities, service offerings and commercial possibilities – factors which are evidently sufficient to make the city more popular as a place to live.

Housing units in Paris, 1994, Philippe Gazeau

How does one live in the generic city? What consequences does the shift in our perception of the city and a new interpretation of distance have for its constituent elements, the apartments and housing typologies? Will this development bring about new typologies or will the existing building fabric undergo successive phases of conversion? What typological qualities and characteristics ensure the long-term sustainability of a typology?

The metamorphosis of the city

At present the city is unable to respond appropriately to this new-found popularity. Since the turn from the 20th to the 21st century, the city has developed into a system for the segregation of different functions. With industrialisation, work areas and residential areas were increasingly separated. After the energy crisis, an increased awareness of healthy environments led to the successive removal of small-scale producers (e.g. butchers, bakers, joiners and carpenters), often unnecessarily, from residential areas because of the emissions and pollution they produced. As segregation increased, so too did the size of the functional units themselves. Competition between hyper- and supermarkets led to new forms of retail which, due to their size, often relocated to the edges of the city. As a consequence, the inner cities began to be seen as a less desirable economic location and suffered accordingly. In addition, in most dense residential areas, the property market has led to a segregation of different social milieus with the result that fewer mixed-use or mixed-type structures have since been built.

The traces of this process of segregation can be seen everywhere: mono-functional structures with business and office buildings are interspersed with a few select residential buildings, mostly for well-heeled residents. The less attractive residential areas erected during the 1970s at the edge of the city and in monotonous residential districts are now largely obsolete and have either been redeveloped or even demolished.

Infill strategies that aim to increase the density of existing urban areas remain politically contentious. However, a large number of urban wastelands are becoming available for new uses: former rail freight depots, military barracks and all manner of derelict industrial sites open up possibilities for redevelopment, radically changing the nature of the urban environment. The development of urban structures on such sites makes it possible to counteract the principles of selection and segregation, and necessitates an examination of complex hybrid structures. Integration, networking and principles of cybernetic interaction replace the previous patterns of urban planning.

The metamorphosis of society

Like the city, so too is society undergoing a process of transformation. The changing structure of employment, a result of globalisation, has led to a restructuring of conventional family patterns. Families now live in different cities, countries or even continents. The term "family" no longer refers only to grandchildren, parents and children but also to patchwork families, step families and single-parent families, communal house or flat sharing or even groups of people who "cohabit" for certain phases in their lives. These new communal structures are in part a result of a shift in the perception of distance towards one another mentioned earlier. Distance creates space – figuratively speaking a reflection of the needs of the inhabitants to find unoccupied niches, to have options – and these in-between spaces need to find an expression in built form. It is this invisible, flexible, empty space that becomes a basis for communal living and thereby also for individual existence. This applies equally to interpersonal space as it does to urban space. The individualisation of the home, the provision of different types of apartments within a building and the combination of houses to create an open environment are architectural options that can lead to new forms and ways of organising the city. Temporary and transitory uses and functionally neutral spaces will shape urban development to a much greater degree than ever before.

New communication and media technologies are increasingly bringing together the realms of living and work. Closed and rigidly defined living spaces and room sizes obstruct this trend while open building structures allow one to better utilise such new potential.

The increasing ageing of the population generates new models for living in a neighbourhood. Houses and apartments in which different generations live together foster opportunities to help one another and exchange services. They offer, alongside the institutionalised models of care and nursing homes, a new form of living in old age that is oriented around an individual way of life. The architecture of this kind of housing must offer a platform for such open forms of communal interaction. Open access and circulation structures linked to semi-public and public spaces have the potential to become spaces for such interaction. The communal aspect could become a catalyst for new forms of housing, as the communal cohabitation of several generations necessitates multi-functional, flexible structures that can be expanded or reduced as required without the need for building works. Such multi-functional and flexible structures should also be ecological and economical, and contribute to the local community in their urban context.

Multi-optional typologies

The metamorphosis of the city and of society has as yet not had an impact on residential housing. Large mono-functional, multi-storey residential blocks remain a cornerstone of the property market, and although there is evident need for multi-optional typologies, a shift in thinking is proving difficult to bring about.

For more than 50 years since the Second World War, the multi-storey apartment block has been and still is the most widespread form of residential housing. It characterises the nature of housing estates, whether arranged in rows or perimeter blocks, as well as the agglomerations of the "Zwischenstadt" ("city without city"). The desire for private outdoor space not overlooked by neighbours, and for a house with views on all sides, and therefore detached, remains the idealised notion of the home. Occasional attempts have been made to seriously interpret and translate these needs into the third dimension and to derive urban structures from this model, but they have rarely attracted any attention in the mass of urban activities.

Privacy and community need to find new forms of expression in housing. Future building structures must be able to accommodate these opposing poles and to interpret them spatially. Such an interpretation is a spatial network of large and small units that are arranged at different densities in an interdependent structure. Positive volumes generate negative volumes which can serve both as recreational space and as space for interaction. Differentiations in the use of levels and volumes of a building structure can be used to create areas with different degrees of intimacy and public-private usage which can serve different functions. With this kind of system, a closed apartment is just as possible as an open arrangement of spaces of different sizes and densities which can be used for interaction or for withdrawal. The building structure is flexible so that it can be adapted to accommodate communal groups of various sizes with different needs and different societal, cultural or sociological orientations. The structure is additionally determined by concepts of cybernetics and autonomy, which are described in more detail in the volume on "row houses" in this series of residential building typologies. In addition to an attractive mixture of residential types with regard to size and orientation, the urban and interactive environment plays a significant role. Generously proportioned and openly accessible circulation and access spaces, which foster interaction and can be used as communal spaces, are just as necessary as carefully designed outdoor areas.

The quality of living spaces is determined by several different factors: proximity to the centre, ease of access, a mixture of historical and contemporary elements and of large and small scales. Well-illuminated interiors and direct sunlight, sufficiently large loggias and a well-proportioned succession of spaces are as much part of the economics of space as contemporary, energy-efficient technical installations. The characteristic qualities of an arrangement of spaces are derived from their different functions and are the product of a symbiosis of cultural, everyday, commercial, ecological, formal and informal considerations.

This mixture, itself a mirror of the realities of society, is not adequately catered for by current residential housing. This critique refers not only to the size of individual dwellings and apartments and the mono-functional structure of residential buildings but also to an attitude fundamentally characterised by a functionalist predilection. Living spaces serve both stimulation and seclusion and have not only purely functional but also emotional aspects. Today, living spaces serve as an extension of the self and an expression of individual personality. Accordingly, the functions of living spaces should not be predefined and the sizes of rooms should allow them to be interchangeable. By providing more than the minimum amount of technical installations and access options, flats and dwellings can be combined and the size of dwellings can be changed by simply coupling spaces together.

The metamorphosis of the city and of society can therefore bring forth new housing typologies. With regard to future urban design, one should also consider traditional urban design issues the other way around, from the viewpoint of housing typology: What demands does an individual dwelling place on the city? How do I design and change the quarter with regard to the building form? What implications does an individual room have for the building form?

Opportunities for the city
This line of inquiry opens up unexpected potential for urban design and offers a new vision of urbanism which Kees Christiaanse has described in his publication *The City as Loft*. The loft originally represents a prototypical, functionally non-deterministic space. After the withdrawal of industry from the industrial quarters of many large American cities, a subculture arose that breathed new life into these high spaces. The principle of the loft departs from the functionalism of Modernism. Instead of defining spaces according to different activities such as sleeping, cooking, eating or living, the loft em-

bodies the principle of integration: everything is one space. Living is every-where. In the one space there are zones, niches and fluid transitions. Furni-ture and flexible insertions structure the space rather than subdividing it.

Christiaanse uses this term to describe a new strategy within the urban context: appropriable, powerful tectonic spaces with high-quality and, abo-ve all, flexible and open living structures. Given the many, sometimes contra-dictory demands a dwelling is expected to fulfil in the generic city described earlier, this may well offer a sustainable strategy for the future.

"Urbane Living 1", 2001, abcarius + burns architecture design

The typology of the town house

The Italian urban villa of the Renaissance is an important testimony to the social milieu of the time.[1] The rooms have more than one door, some have two doors, others three or even four doors. Wherever there was an adjacent room, there was a door. The villa was an assembly of a series of individual interconnected rooms. As with almost all domestic architecture prior to 1650, the Italian urban villa made no qualitative distinction between the path that leads through the building and the rooms for living in. Corridors and stairs simply passed through one room to the next and never served a distinct circulation function. The paths of the inhabitants inevitably crossed and any activity in a room was subject to interruption. Privacy was not accorded great importance. The predilection for social gregariousness, closeness and coincidence of the time appears to correspond to the pattern of circulation and access.

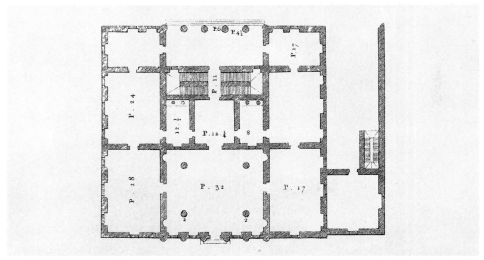

Palazzo Antonini in Udine, 1556, Andrea Palladio

In the 16th century, a room with many doors was regarded as pleasant; by comparison, if one examines a floor plan from the 19th century, there is usually only one door per room. The small number of doors is conditioned by a new form of living together. To reduce the necessary contact between members of a household, access corridors were introduced that were independent of the rooms.

The corridor as a separate space for circulation that kept "traffic" out of the living rooms was first introduced in England in the 16th century. A central corridor connected all the rooms and stairs with one another. The entrance hall, a large flight of stairs, corridors and back stairs formed an extensive network of circulation spaces. A door in each room connected it with a corridor or entrance hall. The architect Sir Roger Pratt was of the opinion that a system of passageways throughout the entire house ensured that one need no longer interrupt work in the servants' rooms by constantly having to pass through them. At this time the corridor was not the only circulation route, but existed parallel to a series of interconnected rooms.

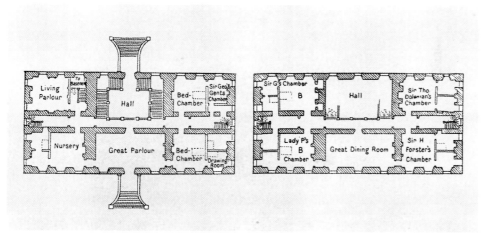

Coleshill House in Berkshire, circa 1650, Sir Roger Pratt

The introduction of the corridor in floor plans had consequences for the way in which one lived together: "Commodity and delight, utility and beauty, function and form"[2] began to diverge into independent categories, heralding a new definition of privacy much as we know it today. The corridor is not solely the product of new floor plans aimed at raising the quality of living but also derives from a growing distinction between the individual and society. As the desire for privacy increased, the corridor offered a strategy of separation combined with a means of providing general access to all rooms.

Since the middle of the 19th century, the form of the corridor as a means of access has remained fundamentally unchanged. The need for a system of spatially distinct rooms is a generally recognised standard in domestic floor plans and with it the need for a separate circulation zone. For the most part, Modernism's contribution was to isolate and individualise people still further.

To comprehend the typology of the town house, it is essential to consider the strategy of circulation and access. The two poles described above – on the one hand, fusion, overlap and simultaneity, on the other separation and functional coding – characterise the spectrum of current floor plan typologies of the town house. New communication technologies and changing societal structures, including manifold forms of cohabitation, themselves often transitory, bring forth new strategies for conceiving space which have parallels with the past. It is the aspect of movement in the floor plan, i.e. the access and circulation typology, that plays a particularly important role.

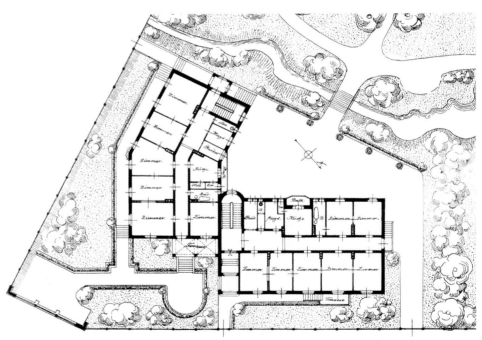

Group of houses in Landsberg an der Lahn, 1906, Hessemer & Schmidt

The most widespread manifestation of the town house arose after the War and is characterised by a few specific recurring patterns of circulation. The most common pattern is a communal staircase with the apartments opening off a central landing. This stairway access type can accommodate two, three or more apartments on each floor. Variants of this type include the addition of an interior corridor, an exterior gallery or a central atrium. This type is rarely used for maisonette apartments with more than one storey. For the most part, the internal organisation of this type of housing is inflexible and functionally predefined. A typical floor plan features a central corridor flanked by rooms on each side, creating a two-sided orientation. It offers little potential for varying the size of the apartment, and these are accordingly typically tailored to the needs of a family with one or two children.

For the most part, the town house typologies shown in this volume eschew this outdated approach, illustrating instead a counter-tendency towards a separated floor plan. The aspects of movement and communication are fundamental to these new typologies: dynamism is the central motif of this architectural concept, which accords movement a role that goes beyond the purely functional aspect of physical access, elevating it to a level of communicative ideology, both in a physical as well as an idealistic sense. We have long been aware of the fact that the world around us is in a state of permanent flux, requiring us to continually change and adapt. Our perception, thinking and actions have become more dynamic. In many scientific disciplines, rigid points of view are no longer sufficient to explain the world around us (see the volume *Row Houses*, "Cybernetics: Integration of type and topos"). The invention of the computer has played a major role in helping us to master these dynamic processes.

The theme of circulation is bound together with the dynamism of the architectural space. The circulation serves to ensure communication between different areas, which are connected with one another in differing degrees of intimacy. Rooms of different shapes and sizes are connected with one another for the purpose of accessibility. The degree of connectivity between the rooms is defined by the path of movement and characterises them as public, semi-private and private spaces. A differentiated elaboration of paths becomes increasingly important, particularly with regard to spaces which can serve multiple purposes, in the sense that they are functionally non-deterministic and can be attributed to different groups of spaces. Paths in separated floor plans should stimulate social interaction and are not solely a functional necessity. Places for interaction and communication, as often cited by architects, are the product of a strategy of multiple superimposition, of pluralistic meaning and functional transparency.

New living patterns, such as single-person households or communal forms of living, give rise to new and dynamic forms of communication and in turn to more open floor plans which in terms of their basic principle resemble the pattern of the aforementioned Renaissance floor plans.

Nevertheless, an enclosed personal space remains a dogma. As everyday life becomes more public, private personal space becomes increasingly important. This tendency is underlined by the fact that many personal spaces now often have a washroom of their own, reachable only from that room. By contrast, many new floor plans no longer feature a separate kitchen. The act of cooking is increasingly seen as being part of living, and what was once a work room is now a social space. The living room, dining room and kitchen are fusing to become a central living area. Bathrooms too are no longer always entirely enclosed. Individual elements such as the bath or shower are increasingly being combined with other rooms. Dark, mono-functional corridors are to be found in very few of the examples in this book. Space for circulation has been reintegrated into the spaces themselves: personal spaces often open onto living or dining areas which have assumed a central distributing function, or the corridor also serves as a dressing or storage area. Similarly, work spaces are also used as distribution zones.

One can observe that circulation has been integrated into the floor plan and is no longer channelled separately. The floor plans of town houses are becoming more open, and designers will be reminded of approaches to free-flowing plans from the age of Modernism: for example Adolf Loos[3], who with his concept of "Raumplan" propagated an open concept of space, arranged spaces on different levels and did not view them as having to be on one common floor. In his concept of "Raumplan", spaces have not only different sizes according to their purpose and meaning but also different heights. Loos composed a series of interrelated spaces into a harmonious, inseparable whole.

Other architects in the same period were also striving to overcome the rigid conventions of traditional house plans. Flowing spaces were already evident in Frank Lloyd Wright's[4] group of prairie houses built in 1893. A conspicuous horizontal arrangement with wide projecting eaves smoothened the progression from inside to outside. In successive phases of development, Wright elaborated his principle of flowing space, creating a series of interconnected spaces without built enclosures to form a spatial continuum that extended out as directly as possible into the surrounding landscape.

The principle of flowing space has been realised particularly rigorously by Gerrit Rietveld in the Schröder House built in 1924, by Richard Neutra in almost all the houses he built from 1927 onwards and by Ludwig Mies van der Rohe in his German Pavilion built for the 1929 Barcelona World Exposition, in which he demonstrated a new conception of space within a geometric arrangement: on top of a plinth, he placed a composition of covered and open spaces to form a flowing whole of interconnected spaces. Space flows around horizontal and vertical planes which do not intersect. The interior and exterior space is treated according to the same principle. A closed volume no longer exists. The built space is as open and directionless as natural space.

A review of archetypical fluid spaces would not be complete without Le Corbusier's concept of the "promenade architecturale"[5]. Movement around, within and through a building plays a central role in his thinking. For Le Corbusier "form" was an active, dynamic and tangible force that breathed life into the system of a building. This is particularly apparent in his design for the Villa Savoye, in which he created a route that led through a regular volume, connecting on its way rooms of different sizes and concentration.

German Pavilion in Barcelona, 1929, Ludwig Mies van der Rohe

These Modernist approaches[6] to superimposition and simultaneity[7] extended and differentiated a concept of space that was already evident in the floor plan of the Italian urban villa. The structural dependencies of the flow of space are made evident. The flow of space in the floor plan must have a corresponding expression in exterior space. The space that surrounds an apartment should relate to the interior and vice versa. This relationship can be observed in the town house types collected in this volume, in particular in their external access routes and the arrangement of semi-private space around the individual apartments.

Private outdoor space that belongs to the individual apartment plays an important role for town houses. Wherever possible, it should not be overlooked and should receive direct sunlight. Such outdoor space can take the form of a terrace, loggia or roof garden and is a key contributory factor for the attractiveness of an apartment as it imparts the feeling of living in one's own house with garden.

A communal staircase as a central access type is becoming less and less common. In many cases, several different access forms are used in combination within one building in order to give inhabitants the feeling that each has their own individual entrance. Some apartments are even accessed via a kind of "vertical front garden", arranged as a loggia between the public staircase and the entrance to the apartment. A further tendency in this context is the extension of the public road up into the upper storeys to provide private parking spaces for the inhabitants' vehicles. This can be seen as an extension of the character of the single-family house into the third dimension.

Residential streets in multi-storey buildings with niches and personalisable space or staircases as communal spaces for meeting and interaction are not necessarily new ideas. Herman Hertzberger has examined the conditions and prerequisites for these kinds of semi-private spaces over many years and has succeeded in incorporating them in his designs repeatedly. In *Lessons for Students in Architecture*[8] he describes how such communal spaces can come about. Increasing the width of a corridor is not sufficient to turn a circulation space into a communicative space. Hertzberger explains how it is necessary to draw subtle boundaries and ensure minimum distances so that spaces result which a resident can personalise. Personalisable spaces in residential schemes are particularly important in large-scale building projects to counteract the anonymity associated with urban ghettos. They also make a major contribution to the general attractiveness of a residential environment.

In view of the fact that individual apartment units in recent town house developments are being arranged closer together to enable them to be coupled, resulting in a greater density and more points of contact for the inhabitants, Hertzberger's lessons are more relevant than ever.

A town house that is built on the principle of communication and movement must unite within it the conflicting requirements of flexibility and specialisation. The new town house types offer their inhabitants a spatial experience that – much like the floor plans of the Italian Renaissance villa – lies between

Space Block Hanoi model, 2003, C+A Coelacanth and Associates

Paul-Clairmont-Straße multi-storey housing, Zurich, 2006, Gmür & Steib Architekten

these poles. The architectural means with which to achieve this are: to activate the access and circulation space; to make more than one means of access possible, both in the floor plan as well as external access; to allow spaces to be used in multiple ways and combinations; and to choose room sizes and proportions so that they do not have to serve a predefined function.

1 see Evans, Robin: "Figures, Doors and Passages", in: *Translations from Drawings to Building and other Essays*. London: AA Publications 1997, p. 55-91

2 Evans, Robin: "Figures, Doors and Passages", in: *Translations from Drawings to Building and other Essays*. London: AA Publications 1997, p. 74

3 see Kulka, Heinrich: *Adolf Loos*. Vienna: Löcker-Verlag 1979

4 see Reed, Peter and Terence Riley (ed.): *Frank Lloyd Wright Architect*. New York: Museum of Modern Art 1994

5 see Curtis, William J. R.: *Le Corbusier – Ideas and Forms*. Stuttgart: Phaidon Press 1992

6 see Kruft, Hanno-Walther: *Geschichte der Architekturtheorie*. Munich: Verlag C. H. Beck 1991

7 see Rowe, Colin and Robert Slutzky: *Transparency*. Basel, Boston, Berlin: Birkhäuser Verlag 1997

8 see Hertzberger, Herman: *Lessons for Students in Architecture*. 3rd updated edition, Rotterdam: 010 Publishers 1998

Floor plan types

In most cases the different types of town houses are characterised by an external access system. Predominant throughout, however, is the tendency to employ a combination of different access typologies within a single project to achieve greater variation. To enable a better comparison of the projects, we have therefore chosen not to employ access typologies but rather spatial categories as our classification system. The categories nevertheless overlap, blend and fuse with one another.

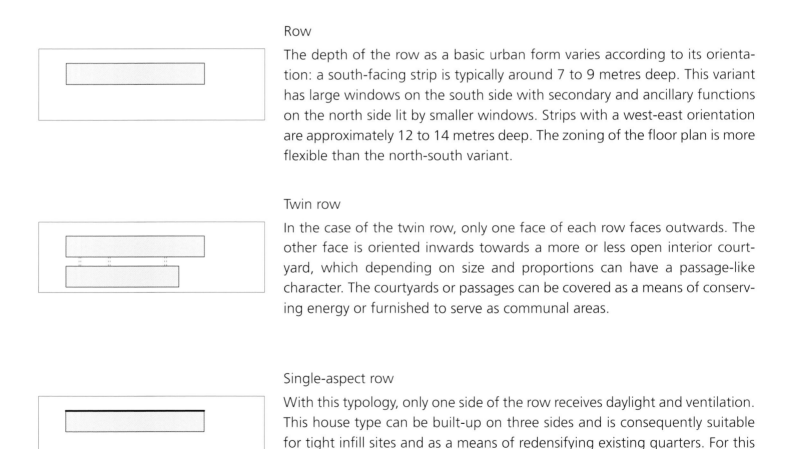

Row

The depth of the row as a basic urban form varies according to its orientation: a south-facing strip is typically around 7 to 9 metres deep. This variant has large windows on the south side with secondary and ancillary functions on the north side lit by smaller windows. Strips with a west-east orientation are approximately 12 to 14 metres deep. The zoning of the floor plan is more flexible than the north-south variant.

Twin row

In the case of the twin row, only one face of each row faces outwards. The other face is oriented inwards towards a more or less open interior courtyard, which depending on size and proportions can have a passage-like character. The courtyards or passages can be covered as a means of conserving energy or furnished to serve as communal areas.

Single-aspect row

With this typology, only one side of the row receives daylight and ventilation. This house type can be built-up on three sides and is consequently suitable for tight infill sites and as a means of redensifying existing quarters. For this reason this typology will in future become increasingly important.

Perimeter block – continuous

The perimeter block is a combination of row and corner floor plans. Its primary typological characteristic is that it faces simultaneously inwards onto an interior courtyard and outwards onto the urban surroundings. Coupled with the need to orient with respect to the sun this results in different floor plan zonings for the respective sides of the block.

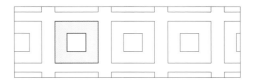

Perimeter block – perforated

This house type is a reaction to the difficult floor plan arrangement of the apartments in the perimeter block. The tension between inward and outward orientation of the floor plan on the one hand and orientation with respect to the sun on the other determine the form of the individual sides of the block. The perforation of the perimeter building is a strategy that creates external spaces and distance between the separate parts of the block.

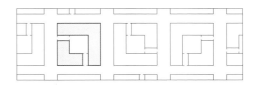

Infill

The infilling of a vacant lot is a traditional design task in the city. The piece that joins together two separate buildings has to accommodate the height and depth of each of its neighbours. In most cases this building has a front-back orientation due to the presence of firewalls on both sides, in some cases, however, it is only single-aspect.

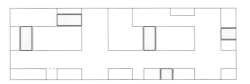

Row
Four storeys
North-south orientation

This programmatic design for a loft house provides a neutral two-storey envelope for the residents to complete according to their own spatial needs. Twelve apartments are accessed via a two-storey platform on the north side, which is constructed as an independent element and connected via bridges. The two-storey envelopes are left as just the shell – only vertical risers and heating are pre-installed – to stimulate the residents to fit them out themselves. Residents are expected not only to add lightweight partitions but also to close off ceiling panels and insert stairs.

The building's façade is likewise conceived with individual personalisation in mind. On the flush south façade, fixed glazing sections alternate with different-sized hinged openings.

The concept of this building is ahead of its time. It demonstrates a new direction in housing and offers homeowners and tenants new spatial potential.

"Kölner Brett" housing
Cologne, 2000
b&k+ brandlhuber & kniess

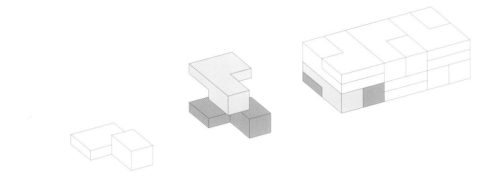

Arrangement of volumes

Longitudinal section

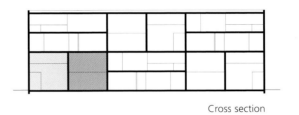

Cross section

Ground floor

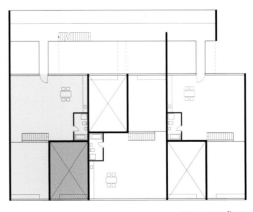

1st upper floor

Row
Four storeys
East-west orientation

At nearly 19 metres, the exceptional depth of this simple arrangement of two flats per floor necessitates an unusual floor plan that allows daylight deep into the building. The west-facing private bedrooms are all of the same width and form a clear barrier to daylight. On the other side, a full-height incision cut deep into the building creates a void with different light qualities which is contained by a large terrace to the east. The resulting floor plan is divided into three narrow strips or zones: an outdoor space with courtyard and terrace, a living and dining area with freestanding kitchen and a further more private section with personal spaces and sanitary facilities. Different room zones result which can be used in different ways: for example, the area near the entrance can serve as a dining or play area. The living room with private spaces at the east end and the large covered terraces create a most contemporary atmosphere for living and working in.

Rhine residence
Basel, 2006
Neff Neumann Architekten

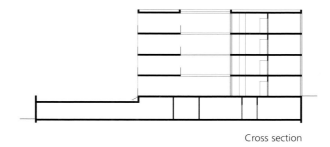

Cross section

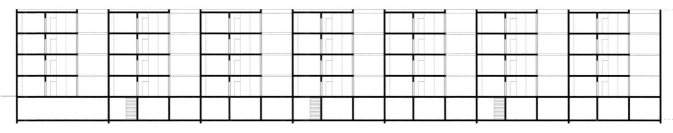

Longitudinal section

Typical floor plan

Row
Four storeys
East-west orientation

This example of an external access gallery arrangement is remarkable in its uncompromising interpretation of the gallery as a space for interaction.

Not only the entrances and kitchens open out onto the gallery but also the living areas, whose generous glazed frontages look onto the wide gallery. Large open sections in the ceiling of the gallery – covered with gridded grating – allow light to penetrate down to the lower floors.

Two more private rooms on the other side of the building face west, of which one is coupled with the living room and can therefore also be used for other purposes. The second bedroom is reached via a corridor that also provides access to a small balcony at the rear. The floor plan can therefore be utilised over its entire depth and allows for a variety of living arrangements. A shift in the alignment of the terraces above the gallery would have afforded each flat greater privacy; but perhaps this was precisely what the designer wished to avoid.

20 apartments
Maastricht, 1995
Wiel Arets Architects

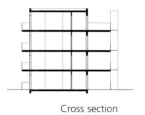

Cross section

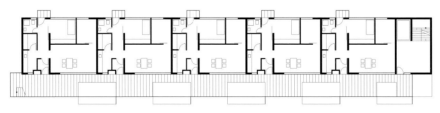

1st upper floor

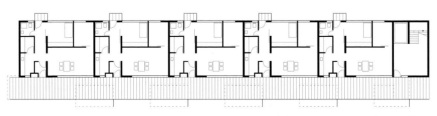

Ground floor

Row
Five storeys
North-south orientation

The more than 200-metre-long row of housing consists of a simple, terraced two-flat-per-floor arrangement with narrow single-flight stairs. This house type consists of three- and four-room apartments which can be enlarged by removing lightweight partitioning walls. The characteristic element of this house type is the arrangement of the loggia. While the bedrooms on the east side feature a continuous loggia, on the west side there are two separate loggias. The living room extends outwards onto a loggia, which is glazed along the street frontage; the bathroom also has a smaller loggia for hanging out the washing.

As each of these elements is clearly articulated as lying in front of the apartment, they give the appearance of independent elements in the urban landscape. The two loggias face one another and also accommodate the change in height resulting from the topography of the site. Because they can be used individually, they set up numerous opportunities for interaction.

Luzernerring housing estate
Basel, 1993
Michael Alder

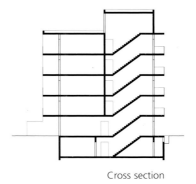

Cross section

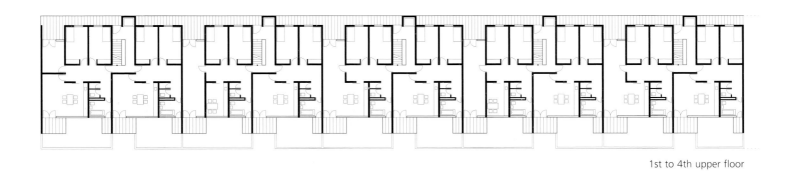

1st to 4th upper floor

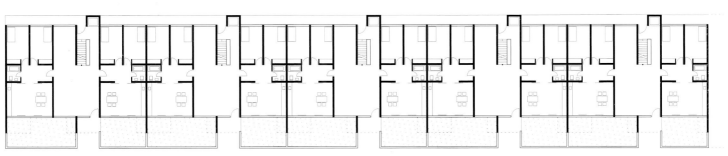

Ground floor

Row
Five to six storeys
East-west orientation

The concept of this row type is simple: the private bedrooms, all of equal size, are neatly arranged next to one another along the east side of the building. An internal circulation zone between the bathrooms and the living rooms makes it possible to simply link bedrooms to the respective living areas. The apartments are reached via a long open gallery along one side that widens in front of the living rooms and entrances to form an outdoor space for each flat.

The sizes of the apartments vary between three and fiverooms. Other combinations are possible by breaking through optional openings at the of the internal circulation zone. Access to the gallery is via an enclosed staircase at one end of the building and an open stair enclosed by the gallery at the other. The building is used as student accommodation. A wider gallery with a more pronounced articulation of the individual zones would make them more attractive for other residential uses.

Bülachhof residences
Zurich, 2003
Marc Langenegger

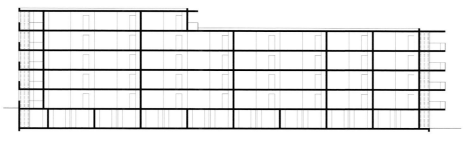

Longitudinal section

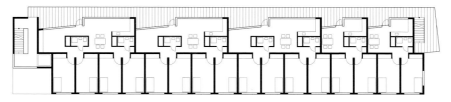

Typical floor plan

Row
Seven storeys
All directions

The meandering figure of this housing scheme consists of north-south and east-west oriented rows of the same depth. The stair access typology serving two flats per floor varies according to orientation: for the north-south rows, the stairwells are arranged parallel to the north side next to the ancillary spaces while all living areas face south. A more private room at the end of the apartment extends the entire width of the building. In the east-west sections, the stairwells are arranged perpendicular to the floor plan, and the apartments accordingly have a twin arrangement of bedrooms, one facing east, the other west. Characteristic for the scheme are the generous loggias that extend deep into the plan and serve in effect as an outdoor room. The deep loggias also represent a model solution for the often problematic northeast corners through the arrangement of all living areas to face the loggia.

Aspholz-Nord residential housing
Zurich, 2005
pool Architekten

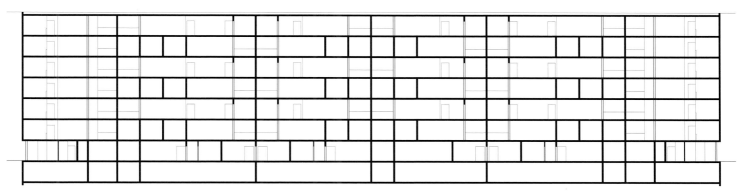

Longitudinal section

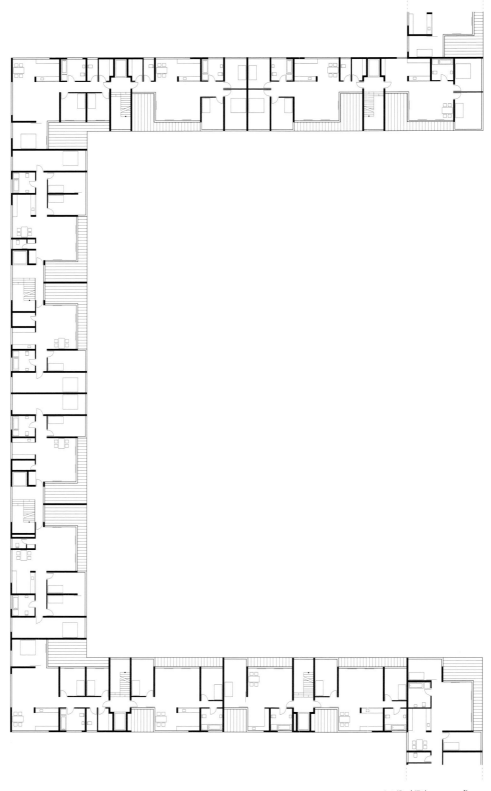

1st/3rd/5th upper floor

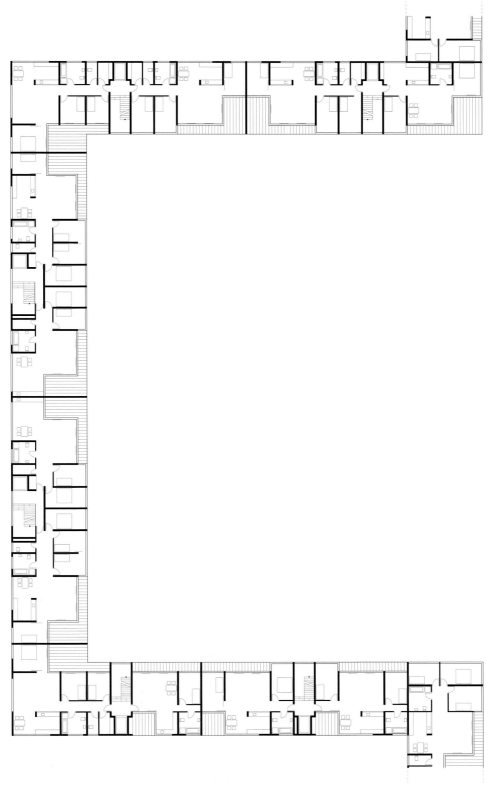

2nd/4th/6th upper floor

**Row
Seven storeys
East-west orientation**

This house type with two flats per floor and a split-level arrangement represents an exception among town houses. The advantages of half-flights of stairs in the centre of the apartment not only reduces the space required for circulation but also creates large one-and-a-half-storey-high spaces.

These spaces all face west so that the lower evening sun can penetrate deep into the floor plan. On the east side, large loggias are arranged in front of the dining areas to benefit from the morning and midday sun. The careful articulation of the loggias, the inter-locking spaces and arrangement of rooms are particular qualities of this housing type. Despite its limitations with regard to disabled access, this kind of split-level housing, which makes good use of passive solar gain, deserves to be employed more often in dense urban contexts.

Aspholz-Süd residential housing
Zurich, 2007
Darlington Meier Architekten

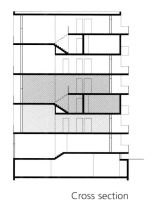

Cross section

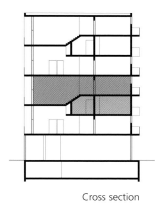

Cross section

1st/4th upper floor

2nd/5th upper floor

3rd/6th upper floor

Row
Eight storeys
East-west orientation

The special feature of this house type is the radical rigour of its formal concept: the principle of a fully-glazed skeleton construction, with regularly articulated columns and floor slabs on the façade, is stringently followed throughout. This skeleton also informs the geometric system of the floor plans.

The overall figure, which is exceptionally deep – splaying outwards still further at each end – consists of a pair of internally positioned stairwells and lifts serving two flats per floor. All living areas, as well as a small toilet with shower, face the fully-glazed frontage. An entrance corridor, internal hallway and a second corridor provide access to each of the separate rooms as well as a bathroom and separate toilet in the centre of the plan. Each loggia is integrated into the façade of the building.

The apartments are appropriately spacious and the full-height glazing connects the interiors with the green park outside most effectively.

Schwarzpark residences
Basel, 2004
Miller & Maranta

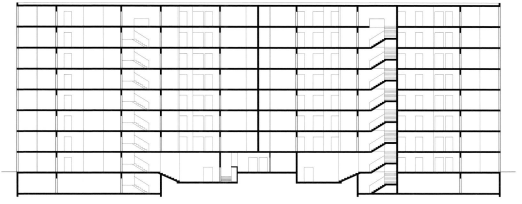

Longitudinal section

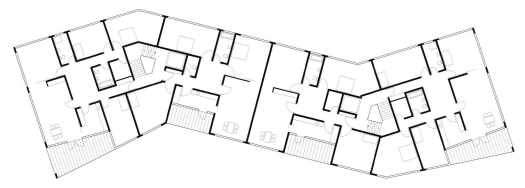

Typical floor plan

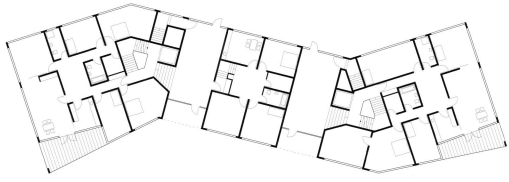

Ground floor

Row
Eight storeys
All directions

The interlocking system of different-sized apartments in this housing complex skilfully combines different maisonette apartments, reached via staircases serving two flats per floor. The result is an exceptionally deep floor plan, a factor of the stepped arrangement of the apartments. Given the depth of 13.5 metres, the architects have been able to achieve a very good proportion of circulation to living space. The vast volume of the buildings in this complex, which cascades down a hilly site reaching in parts seven storeys, are dealt with masterfully. The single-aspect apartments are connected via a single flight of stairs to the next floor where they receive light from both sides. The single-floor apartments have a generous living and dining area that spans the width of the building with a niche for the kitchen fittings. At the ends of the buildings, these rooms open out onto a terrace that likewise utilises the full building width. At roof level the apartments are supplemented by terraces let into the roof. The same floor plan system is used for the one block with a north-south orientation.

Leimbachstrasse multi-storey housing
Zurich, 2005
pool Architekten

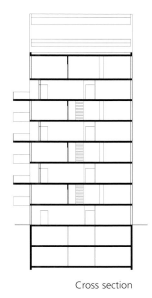

Cross section

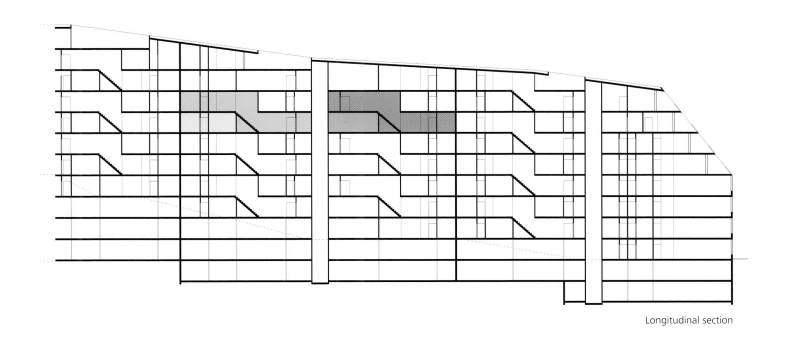

Longitudinal section

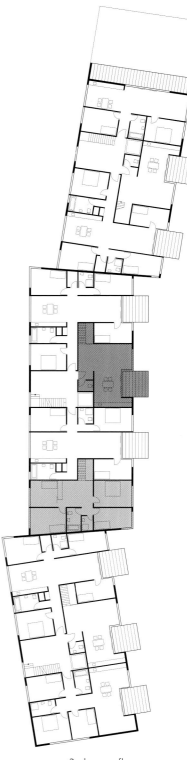

Ground floor

1st upper floor

2nd upper floor

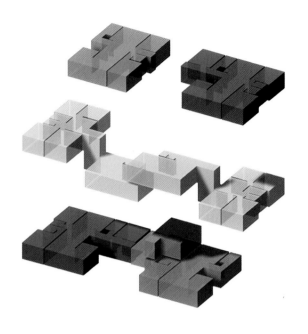

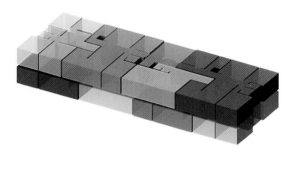

Interlocking arrangement of apartments

Row
Nine storeys
North-south orientation

The strongly delineated housing slab is accessed via a single long outside walkway which is in turn accessed by a single lift. The additional stairs serve as fire escapes and as a means of communicating between the different levels. Except for a few exceptions in the top four storeys, all the apartments follow exactly the same principle: a small entrance zone with bathroom and kitchen behind is fixed, the remaining three rooms are flexible, divided by lightweight sliding partitions, and are laid out with traditional Japanese tatami mats. Each of these rooms has fitted cupboards with tatami dimensions. Two of the rooms are the size of six tatami mats, the third the size of nine mats. An internal corridor passes along the frontage, parallel to the outside walkway, providing access to the rooms.

In the four top storeys, the system is varied with maisonettes. Here the entrances with the kitchens form a double-height gallery space containing the stairs.

Gifu Kitagata apartments
Yokohama, 2000
Akiko + Hiroshi Takahashi workstation

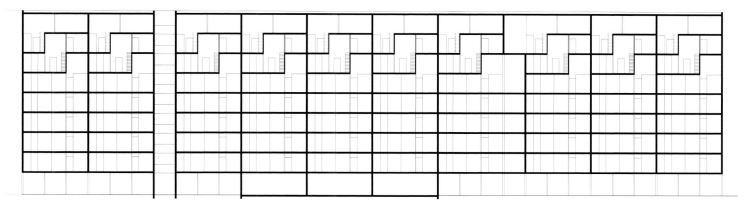

Longitudinal section

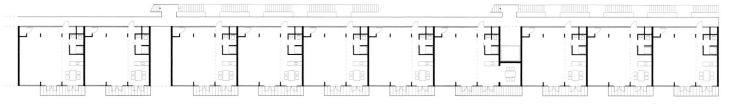

7th upper floor

6th upper floor

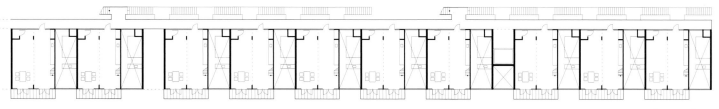

5th upper floor

Row
Three to four storeys
North-south orientation

This building type is inspired by house types from the lagoon city of Venice. In Venice, all houses are required to be accessible from two sides – from dry land and from the water. The pivotal element of this type is a small internal courtyard, which serves as distributor and light well. The building sections arranged around it interact quite differently with the outdoor space. The low-level volume is oriented towards the water, the upright volume to the landward side and better lighting conditions.

Translated to an urban situation, this principle can be used to regulate the illumination for north-south or east-west orientations. The internal access is via a straight single flight of stairs, the illumination partially via light wells. The principle can accommodate different building depths as the internal courtyard in the centre of the plan also provides illumination.

Diploma project
Darmstadt University
Alexander Scholtysek

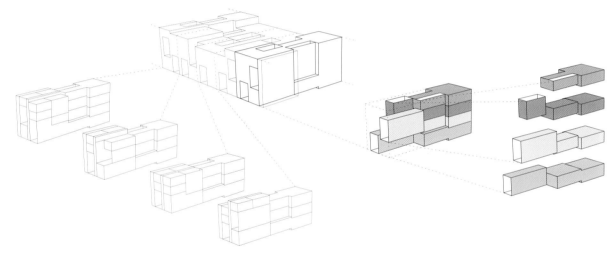

Arrangement of volumes

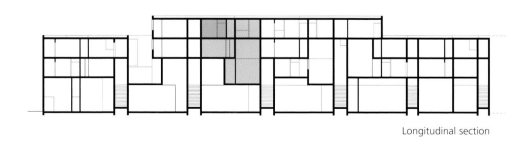

Longitudinal section

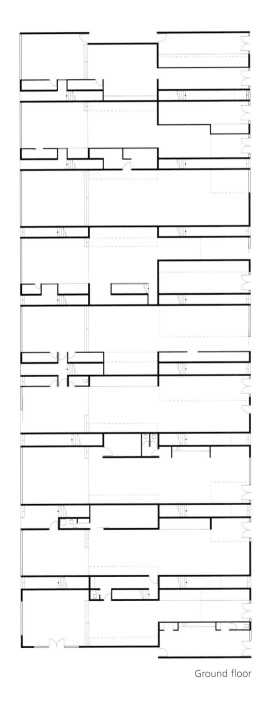

Ground floor

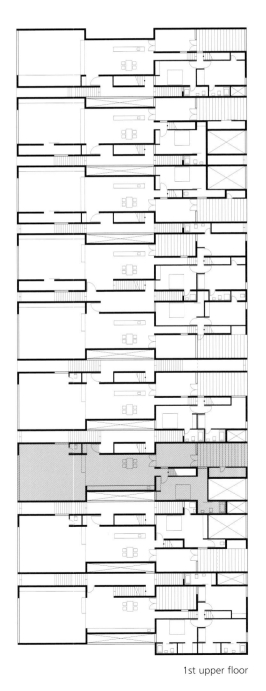

1st upper floor

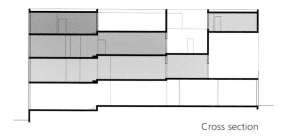

Cross section

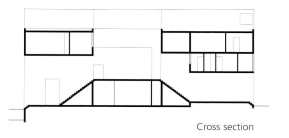

Cross section

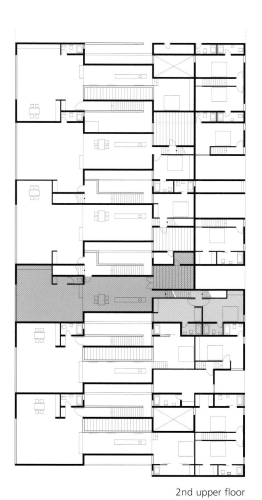

2nd upper floor

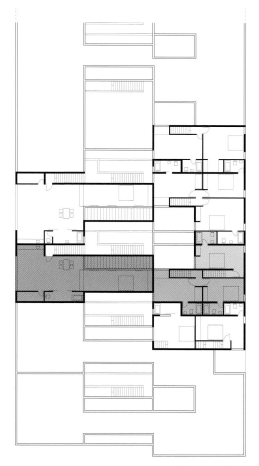

3rd upper floor

Row
Four storeys
North-south orientation

The design is conceived as a way of dealing with extremely deep narrow urban sites. Deep incisions, which widen to become courtyards, help illuminate the elongated house types. A characteristic feature of this house type is its use of single flights of stairs, sometimes ascending four storeys.

The cascade-like arrangement of the stairs above one another makes it possible to create floor plans with a variable number of personal spaces per living area. Each of these personal spaces has its own sanitary facilities and can function autonomously as a one-room apartment. As the openings in the individual units are always offset to one another and look in different directions, it is possible to create very private spaces in close proximity to one another. Open courtyards and galleries, as well as half-height levels in some areas, provide points of rest within the complex constellation of spaces and ensure that even deep rooms are sufficiently illuminated.

Diploma project
Darmstadt University
Eva Martini

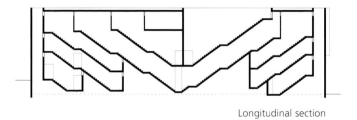

Longitudinal section

Longitudinal section

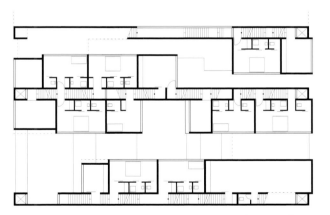

1st upper floor

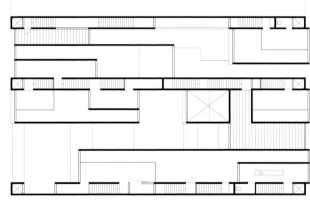

3rd upper floor

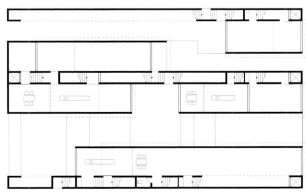

Ground floor

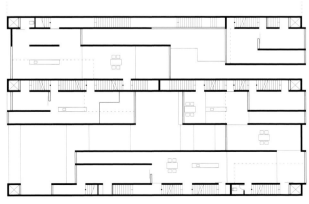

2nd upper floor

Row
Four storeys
North-south orientation

The access system for this north-south oriented row is inspired by a double-helix stair. Two pairs of parallel stairs leading in opposite directions provide access from two sides, in this case from the north and south. The same arrangement with two series of stairs, one behind the other, requires more circulation space but also significantly increases the number of possible combinations of different-sized apartments. The deep building plan is illuminated by additional internal court-yards, which can be deeper or longer to fit the system. Although the house is accessed from either the right or left-hand side only, the system of staircases allow different combinations on the upper storeys and enable one to exploit the full depth of the building. Small and large apartments, single-storey or maisonette, single or dual-aspect are all possible as a result of the arrangement of the doors alone.

Student project
Darmstadt University
Florian Götze

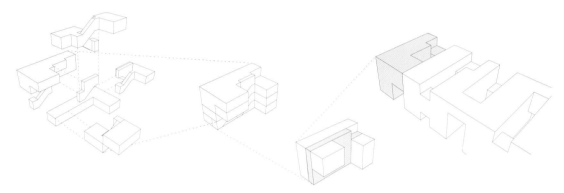

Arrangement of volumes

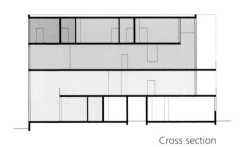

Cross section

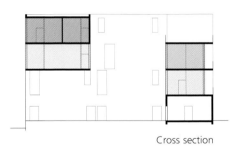

Cross section

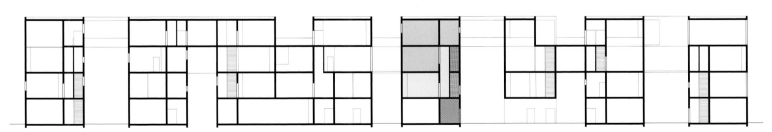

Longitudinal section

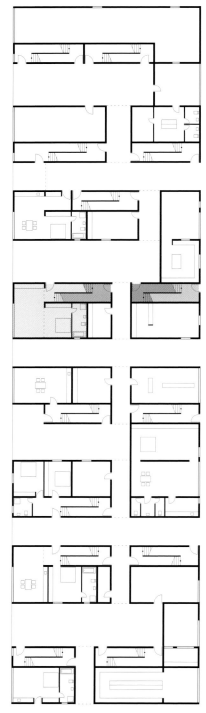

Ground floor

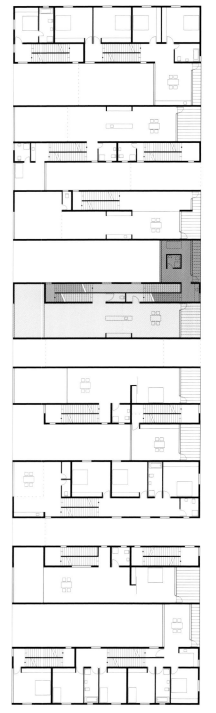

1st upper floor

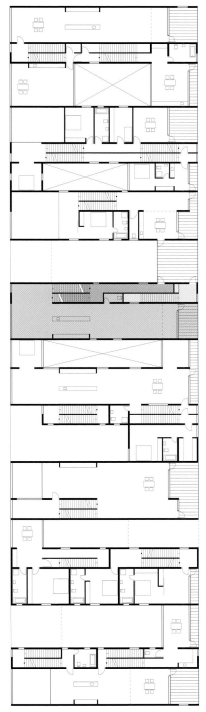

2nd upper floor

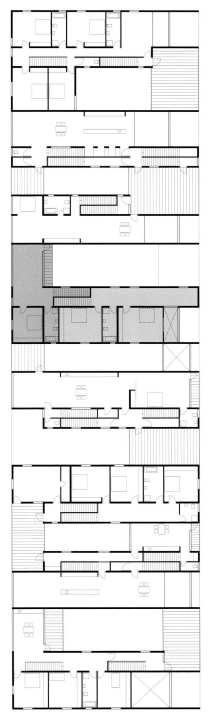

3rd upper floor

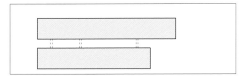

Twin row
Four storeys
East-west orientation

These large-volume clusters are part of a permeable perimeter block and contain up to 30 different apartments depending on the type. All the apartments are accessed from an internal courtyard: the maisonettes in the west wing via staircases, the single-level apartments in the east wing via single flights of stairs which are reached from a raised circulation zone on the first floor. The ground floor level of the east wing contains open car parking spaces in lieu of underground parking.

All apartments have two-storey "energy gardens" that face west or south. This also applies for the more slender single-level apartments in the east wing. Here the energy gardens are arranged offset over two storeys and extend above the roof level on the uppermost storey.

Each of the four approximately equal rooms in the west wing can be used for different purposes. A lift at the end of the cluster provides disabled access for some of the apartments.

IBA twin row
Berlin, 1999
Günter Pfeifer

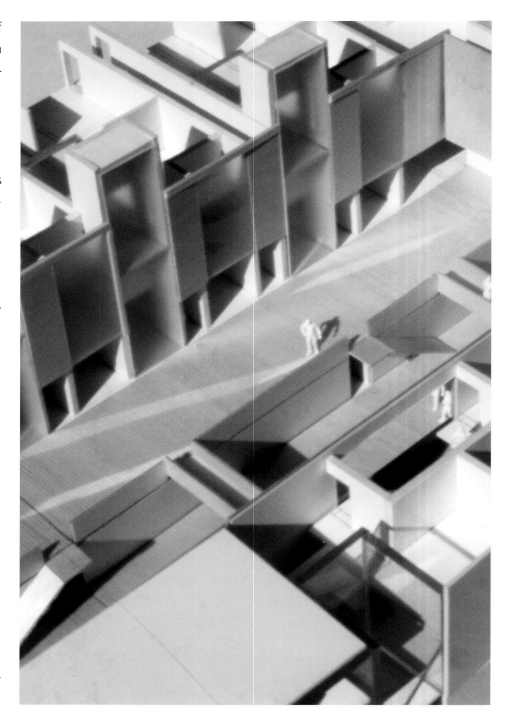

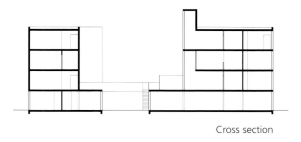

Cross section

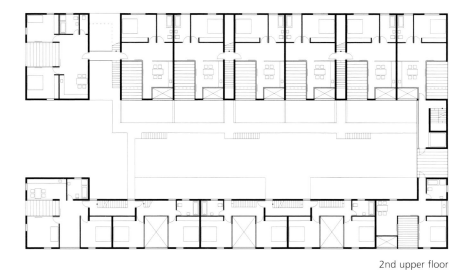

2nd upper floor

1st upper floor

**Twin row
Four storeys
East-west orientation**

The basic urban figure is an interpretation of the traditional "Schlitzhaus" common in Hamburg around the end of the 19th century. Narrow north-south alleys separate the house types into two parallel rows, one facing east, one facing west. The problem of daylight illumination from one side only is resolved through a skilful arrangement of stepped-back terraces on the upper floors. Maisonette apartments have been arranged on the ground floor, which is slightly elevated to reduce overlooking. On the second floor – reached via a stair that feeds three flats per landing and a bridge for the west side – the living rooms with south-facing terraces extend the entire depth of the building. The apartments on the third floor are slightly smaller; the south-facing terrace is arranged so that the neighbours do not feel overlooked. The especially deep twin flat arrangement of the north-south row steps down southwards through the use of terraces; deep cutouts ensure that the house types which face north receive direct light from the east or west at the corners.

Rotherbaum housing estate
Hamburg, 1998
Atelier 5

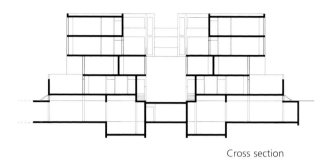

Cross section

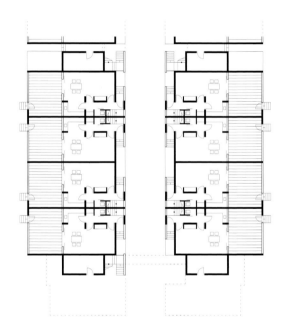

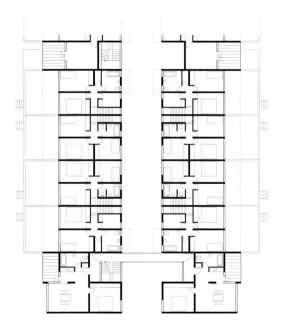

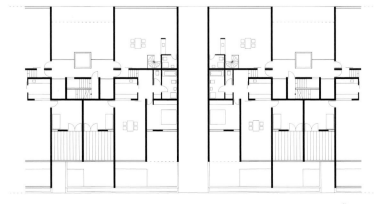

Ground floor

1st upper floor

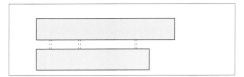

Twin row
Five storeys
East-west orientation

A glass roof covers a five-storey atrium between parallel rows of apartments that face east and west. A series of walkways and bridges provide access to the apartments. Along with the bridges, small terraces in front of the entrances to the apartments help create an atmosphere that encourages inter-action in a space which, thanks to passive solar gain, can be used all year round.

In the apartments on the west side, only the kitchen opens onto the atrium space; on the east side, the living rooms of the apartments extend the entire depth of the row so that these apartments also benefit from light from the west. In addition, the living areas have glazed bays on the east elevation. The mixture of two and three-room apartments in each flank is supplemented by four-room apartments at each end of the row. Through the use of energy-efficient in-stallations and passive technologies, the covered atrium serves as a means of naturally ventilating, heating and cool-ing the building.

Holzstraße housing scheme
Linz, 1999
Herzog + Partner

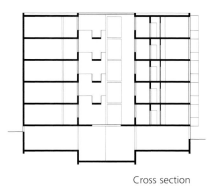

Cross section

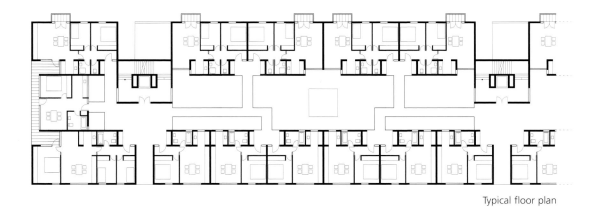

Typical floor plan

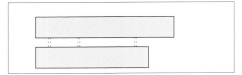

Twin row
Three to four storeys
North-south orientation

This twin row arrangement with access from two sides is designed for inner-city locations. All sides of the ground floor can be used for large-scale retail or office usage. When raised a few steps off the ground, the ground floor can also be used for residential housing.

Access to the upper floor is via two straight, single flights of stairs on opposite sides of the building, which open onto a small, elevated inner courtyard. This courtyard offers an internal space for interaction and affords better natural lighting for the apartments on the upper floors. Depending on the block type, each courtyard provides access to two or three apartments, all of them maisonettes. Some house and floor plan types also have a roof terrace or additional living space on the third floor. A variant with single-storey apartments on the first floor is conceivable when the second-floor apartments are accessed via a stair from the inner courtyard.

Diploma project
Darmstadt University
Valeska Bühler

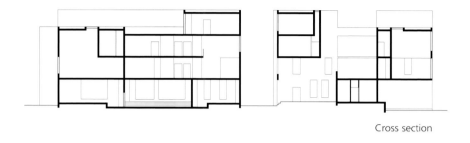

Cross section

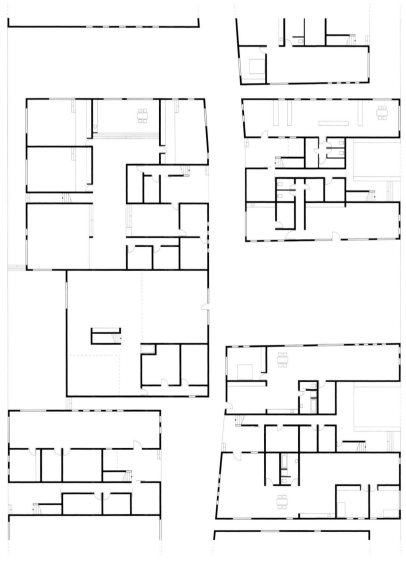

Ground floor

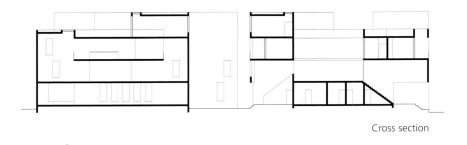

Cross section

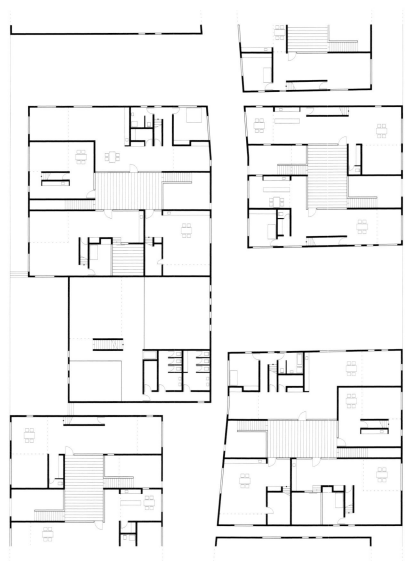

1st upper floor

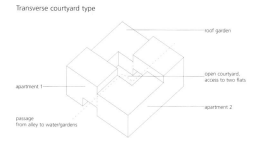

roof garden

open courtyard,
access to two flats

apartment 1

apartment 2

passage
from alley to water/gardens

apartment 1

roof garden

apartment 2

apartment 3

open courtyard,
access to two flats

roof garden

apartment 4

passage
from alley to water/gardens

Block types

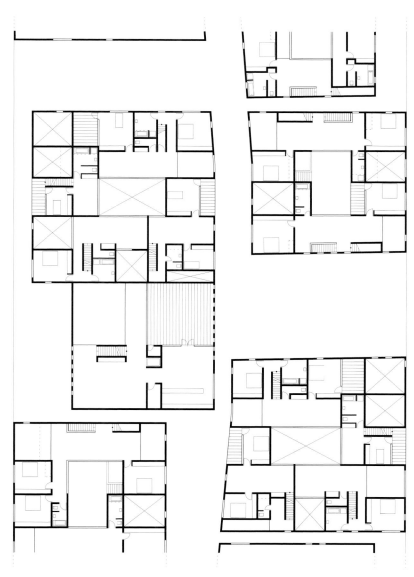

2nd upper floor

Single-aspect row
Five storeys
South orientation

In this single-aspect row of housing, all the apartments have to be accessed from the south. On the ground floor, the slightly raised apartments are accessed directly from the street via short stairs, on the third floor via an elevated walkway reached by an open staircase at each end. The ground floor contains a series of two-storey, equal-sized three-room maisonette apartments. The internal stair to the upper level is arranged as a single flight of stairs at the back of the flat behind the kitchen.

The apartments on the third floor, reached via the walkway, are also maisonettes but of different sizes. Two of the entrances open onto a lobby, each of which provides access to two further apartments: a three-room apartment, which is coupled with the second floor below, and a somewhat larger four-room apartment coupled with the fourth floor above. The stacking of the different apartment types above one another according to the rhythm of the cross walls ensures an economical construction.

Cité Saint Chaumont housing
Paris, 1993
Francis Soler

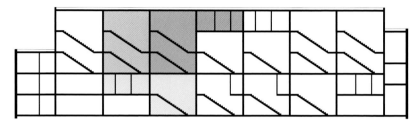

Longitudinal section

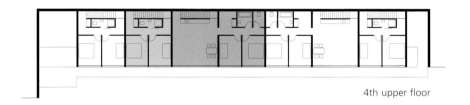

4th upper floor

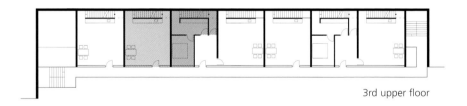

3rd upper floor

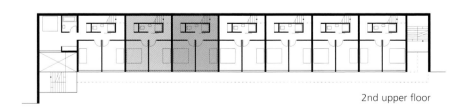

2nd upper floor

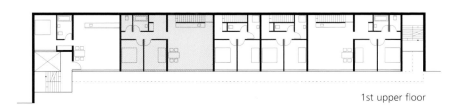

1st upper floor

Single-aspect row
Four storeys
North-south orientation

Inner-city situations can sometimes produce constraints such as those of this housing estate in Berlin, which consists of single-aspect rows of houses with a north or south orientation. To compensate for the lack of daylight in the north-oriented apartments, a series of deep incisions are cut into the volume of the building to allow sun from the east and west to penetrate deep into the floor plan.

The stepping of the volumes and the combination possibilities offered by the two-storey spaces produce a rhythm of rooms that can be coupled in different permutations. The floor plan is divided into three zones: a façade zone with kitchen, dining areas and terraces, a central zone with living areas, bedrooms and circulation, and a third zone with ancillary spaces and rearward lighting courts. Because each section has a stairwell on both sides, each with a front and a rear entrance, the arrangement and succession of the spaces in-between can be divided into different-sized areas simply by closing doorways.

Student project
Darmstadt University
Kathrin Hinkel

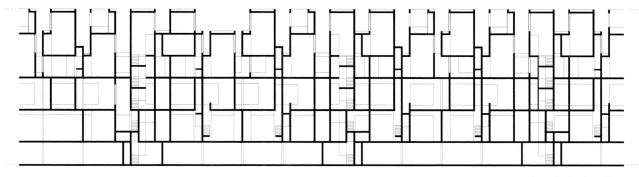

Longitudinal section

3rd upper floor

2nd upper floor

Single-aspect row
Five storeys
North-south orientation

This project employs two approaches to tackle the problem of north-facing single-aspect apartments. Firstly, the floor plan is divided down the middle into spatial zones using a split-level arrangement: living and dining areas face the façade, with bedrooms and bathrooms in the darker rearward zone. Secondly, a deep notch is inserted between the apartments of the north-facing row that extends the height of the three uppermost storeys. These incisions, together with the deep loggias, allow light from the east and west to illuminate the north-facing apartments. The incisions in the row on the south side serve partially as four-storey tower-like apartments. The stepped arrangement of the floors divides the flats into semi-public and private zones. Further lighting courts in the second zone help ventilate the rooms and lend them a special atmosphere of their own. This second layer also has a secondary means of access via the loggia behind the stairwells.

Student project
Darmstadt University
Martin Trefon

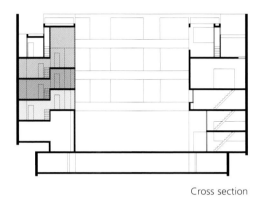

Cross section

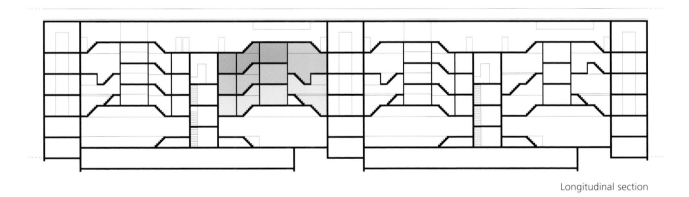

Longitudinal section

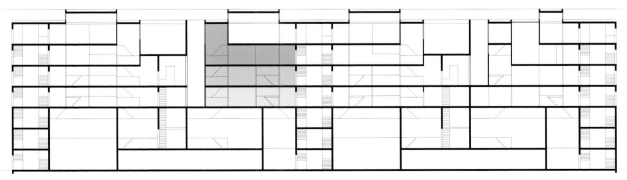

Longitudinal section

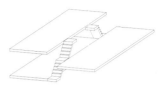

Circulation

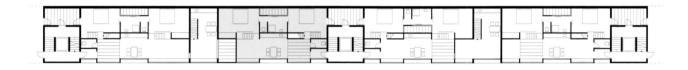

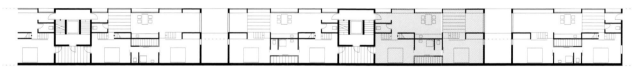

1st upper floor

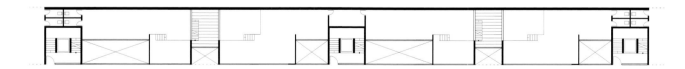

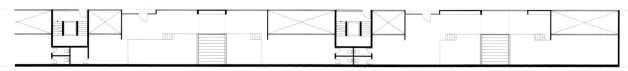

Ground floor

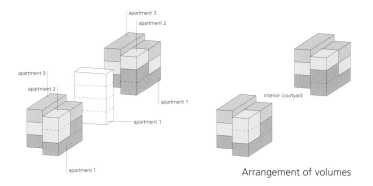

apartment 3
apartment 2

apartment 3
apartment 2

apartment 1

apartment 1

apartment 1

apartment 1

interior courtyard

Arrangement of volumes

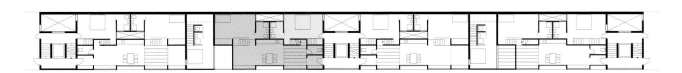

3rd upper floor

2nd upper floor

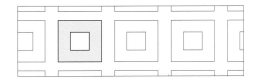

Perimeter block – continuous
Five storeys
All directions

The five-storey block is arranged around a large interior space, partially open to the sky, with an open gallery that provides access to all the apartments. Two enclosed staircases in the gallery contain a cascading series of single-flight stairs and are supplemented by three lifts. Almost all apartments are accessed from one side of the corridor. The diagonal face of the building solves the problem of north-facing apartments, ensuring that these flats receive sufficient light from the west. A special feature of this building is the three 33-metre-long, east-west oriented apartments that extend the depth of the building and include large south-facing roof terraces in the interior of the block.

The luxurious three-room apartments each have two entrances. The remaining floor plans are typical corridor floor plans with sometimes extremely narrow rooms. The apartments on the uppermost floor have an additional roof terrace.

Botania complex
Amsterdam, 2002
Frits van Dongen, de Architekten Cie.

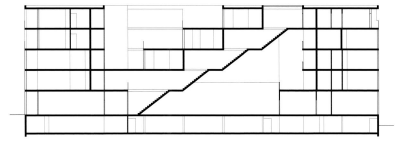

Longitudinal section

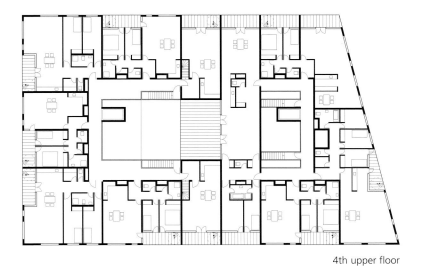

4th upper floor

3rd upper floor

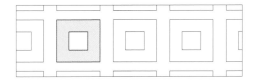

Perimeter block – continuous
Six to seven storeys
All directions

The urban perimeter block is accessed via four internal staircases arranged in the "elbows" of the building. The entrances to the compact staircases open onto the public passageways to the interior courtyard. The entrance on the southeast side is given special prominence by an open entrance platform. The ground floor on the northwest side is used for commercial premises.

With only a few exceptions, all the apartments are three or four-room apartments. As the staircases are arranged in each inner corner, two apartments are reached via a small access gallery that looks out over the courtyard. The small flats reached via the gallery are, with one exception, two-room apartments. The generous loggias on the corners of the building are particularly apparent and together with the corner glazing of the living room lend the building a striking appearance. The loggias facing the interior courtyard project beyond the façade like balconies, facilitating active interaction between the inhabitants.

Nordlyset residences
Copenhagen, 2006
C. F. Møller Architects

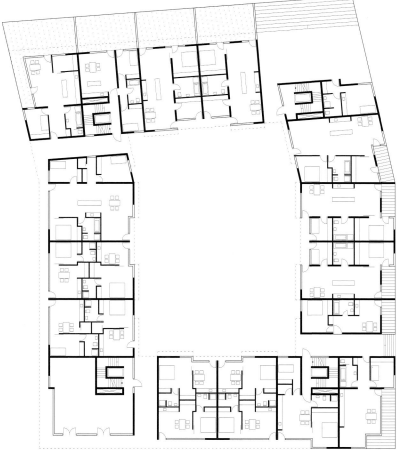

Ground floor

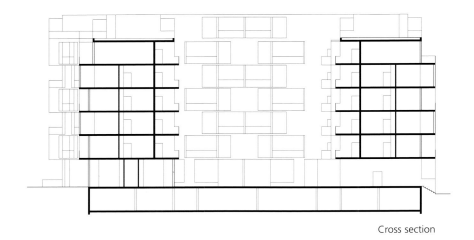

Cross section

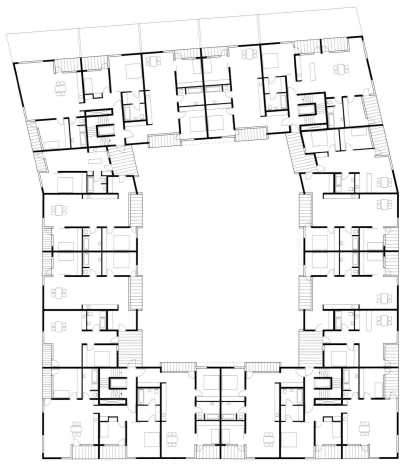

1st/3rd/5th upper floor

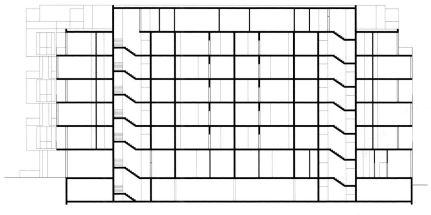

Cross section

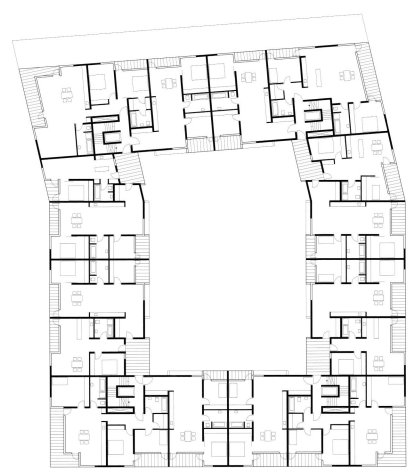

2nd/4th upper floor

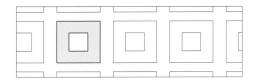

Perimeter block – continuous
Four storeys
All directions

The basic idea of this design is an alternating arrangement of private spaces around communal areas of differing degrees of privacy: within the flats themselves and between the flats and public spaces which are part of the entire residential complex. Different apartment sizes and plans are possible. Each "Cocooning Module" contains a washroom, a living and sleeping area and a loggia in addition to a small kitchen unit. The individual modules can be arranged in rows, connected by communal areas, and can be coupled to form different-sized apartments.

The various courtyard forms result from the differing illumination and access methods and, as public spaces, facilitate a maximum degree of interaction. This design is envisaged as a model for new ways of living, such as for patchwork families or as communal housing for a mix of different age groups.

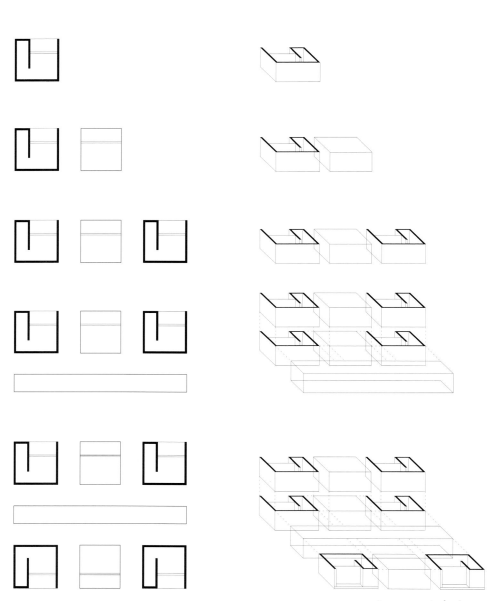

Arrangement of volumes

Student project
Darmstadt University
Angèle Tersluisen

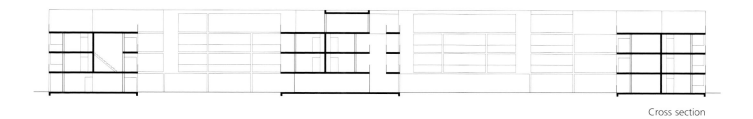

Cross section

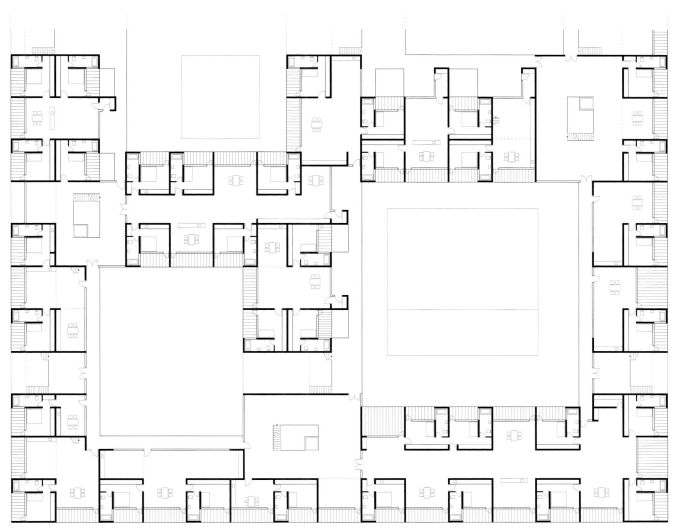

2nd upper floor

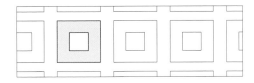

Perimeter block – continuous
Six storeys
All directions

In the Berlin neighbourhood of Prenz-lauer Berg, one can still find perimeter block structures with a succession of interior courtyards. This project takes the rigorous arrangement of internal courtyards as its theme, transforming them with a view to improving the quality of living in the dense interior space of the courtyard.

The stairs and lifts are arranged in the dark intersections of the typology and lit naturally from above via a skylight and stairwell. All the apartments are two-storey maisonettes with an entrance from the staircase on each floor, in accordance with Berlin regulations.

The apartments are accessed from their innermost corner. A loggia extending the depth of the building adapts the maisonette character by employing a stepped arrangement of the storeys and ensures that the flats in the courtyards receive sufficient daylight. Each block contains different-sized apartments according to their location. If desired, the maisonette apartments can be divided into two smaller single-storey apartments.

Student project
Darmstadt University
Annika Kingl

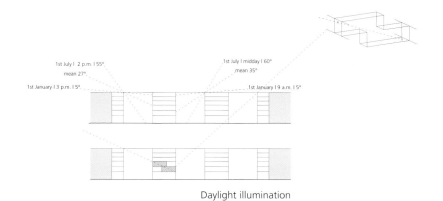

1st July | 2 p.m. | 55°
mean 27°
1st January | 3 p.m. | 5°

1st July | midday | 60°
mean 35°

1st January | 9 a.m. | 5°

Daylight illumination

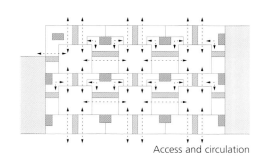

Access and circulation

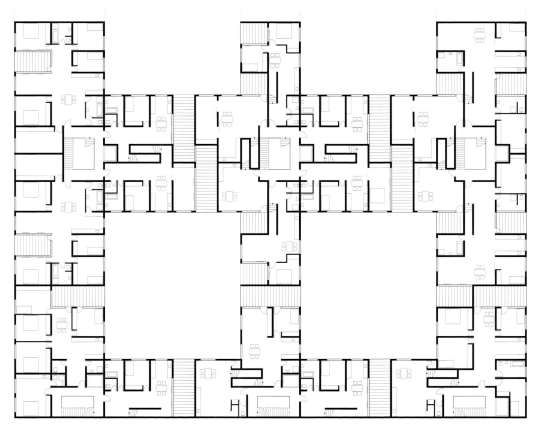

1st/3rd upper floor

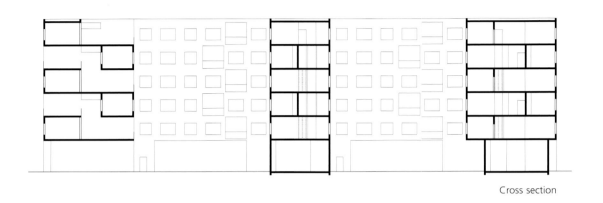

Cross section

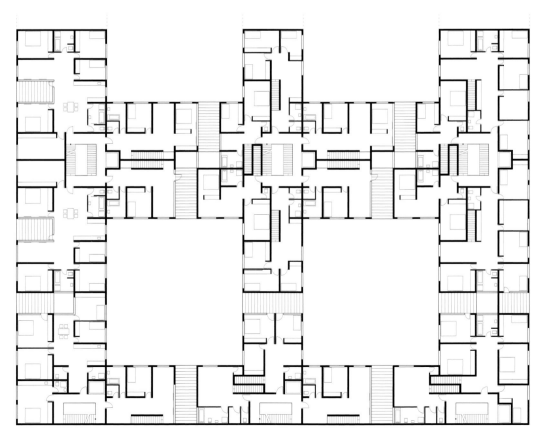

2nd/4th upper floor

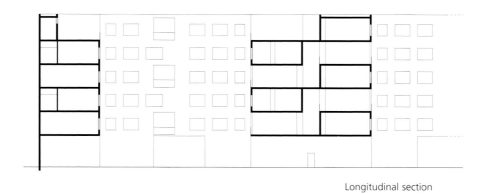

Longitudinal section

5th upper floor

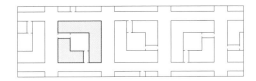

Perimeter block – perforated
Three storeys
All directions

The three-storey housing complex is bounded by a common roof and accessed exclusively via the interior courtyard. Accordingly, the interior of the block is a vibrant space for interaction, with spacious lawns, planting and play areas. Typologically, the apartments are more akin to row houses, with access to the ground floor from the courtyard, to the first floor via a stair and terraces and to the top floor via long, broad gallery walkways.

The three-room house types on the ground and first floors are divided into a more public and a more private zone through the placement of the bathroom in the centre and the connector-corridor. The top floor apartments are small but well-proportioned two-room apartments. A sliding partition allows the top apartments to be used in various ways; both rooms open out onto the large loggia beneath the roof.

Rotterdamer Straße housing complex
Düren, 1997
Herman Hertzberger

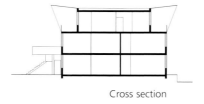

Cross section

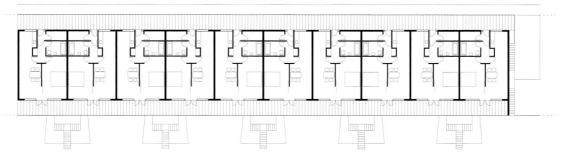

Top floor

1st upper floor

Ground floor

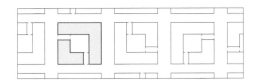

Perimeter block – perforated
Three storeys
All directions

This three-storey housing development consists of a system of two different house types – a long north-south oriented block and three east-west oriented buildings – which are repeated and mirrored.

The floor plans of the north-south block are clearly divided into south-facing living areas with ancillary spaces and circulation to the north. The maisonette apartments have an optional stair to the top floor making it possible to create either a large three-storey apartment or a separate living area on the top floor. This top flat has its own entrance via an elevated walkway.

The three communal staircases provide access to the upper gallery as well as to the three east-west buildings. The typology of the apartments in the east-west oriented buildings feature an entrance hallway along one side which is wide enough to serve as a living or play area. The living and dining rooms with kitchen at the north end of the building are also connected to large open terraces which face south back into the courtyard.

Vogelbach housing development
Riehen, 1992
Michael Alder

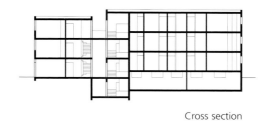

Cross section

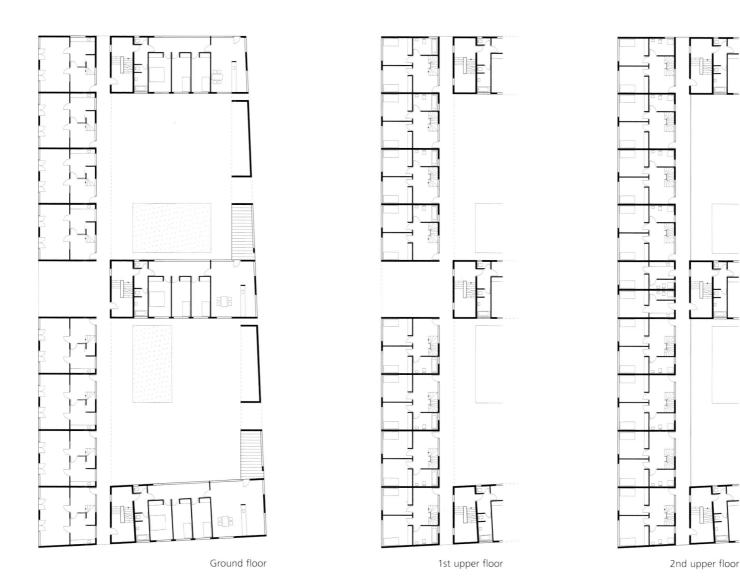

Ground floor

1st upper floor

2nd upper floor

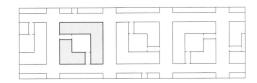

Perimeter block – perforated
Five storeys
All directions

A particular characteristic of this housing complex is its unusual means of access. On the ground floor, entrance is via several courtyards arranged along the length of the comb-shaped complex. External stairs ascend several storeys, leading along two buildings to the south, passing through the third floor to an internal walkway on the fourth floor. On the first floor, access to the four-room maisonettes, which switch over to the north side on the second floor, is from the rear. Half-landings on the north side provide access to interlocking maisonettes that switch back from the second floor to the first floor. An internal walkway on the fourth floor provides access to the remaining apartments, which are similarly coupled with the floor below to form maisonettes. This system of access produces apartments with unusual floor plans. Because they make use of both east and west orientation, they are particularly well-lit.

Void/hinged space housing complex
Fukuoka, 1992
Steven Holl Architects

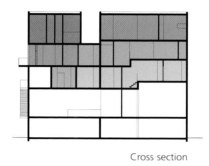

Cross section

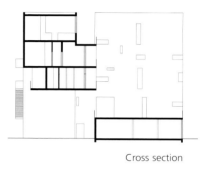

Cross section

2nd upper floor

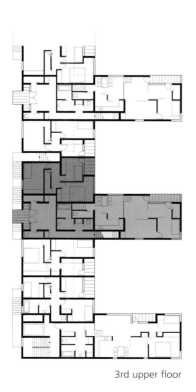

3rd upper floor

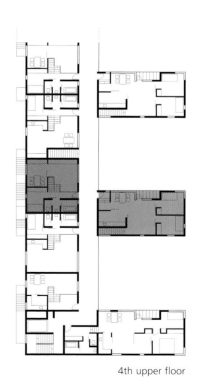

4th upper floor

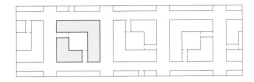

Perimeter block – perforated
Seven storeys
All directions

The main typological characteristic of the floor plans in this partially enclosed perimeter block is to ensure sufficient daylight illumination for all the apartments given their inner-city location. Staircases provide access to four apartments per landing with a combination of different maisonettes on the upper storeys. The standard situation on the third and fourth floors features two apartments with open living areas and a large open terrace as well as a third inward-facing maisonette apartment on the west side. The luxurious apartments on the sixth floor are maisonette apartments, each with two large terraces. Although they follow a conventional six-room arrangement, they serve as generous four-room apartments due to the gallery space adjacent to the central living area. Compared with the generous sizes of the terraces and rooms, the toilets and bathrooms in the centre of the plan are small. The apartments in the side wings are smaller and have no loggias.

81 housing units
Paris, 1997
Philippe Gazeau

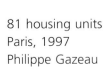

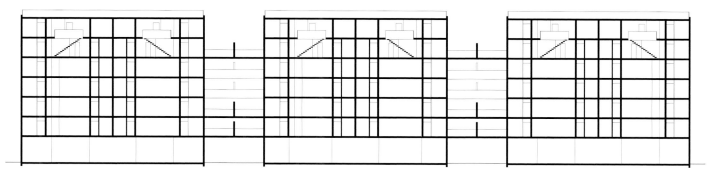

Longitudinal section

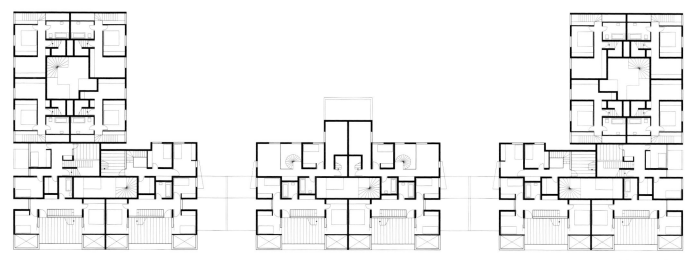

6th upper floor

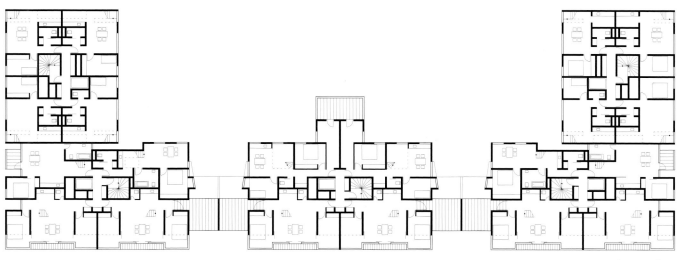

5th upper floor

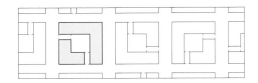

Perimeter block – perforated
Five storeys
All directions

Intergenerational housing is the product of a search for forms of housing that support a sense of community while catering for a variety of different ways of life. For this, both floor plans as well as the building arrangement need to be variable. The concept shown here uses a two-storey distributor, or hub, which can serve as an extended communal space for living or dining in. Private rooms, each with their own sizeable bathroom, are attached to this as modules for individual ways of living, working, sleeping and, to a limited degree, also cooking.

Each cluster can have a different combination of communal spaces and private modules – 1+5, 2+4, 3+3. The lower and ground floors can house communal functions, such as child care, a swimming pool, relaxation and shopping. Sunlight and illumination can be varied as desired according to location: in the peaceful inner courtyard, the louder urban courtyard or the passageway.

Student project
Darmstadt University
Janna Jessen

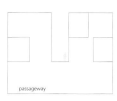

passageway

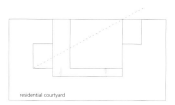

residential courtyard

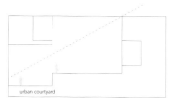

urban courtyard

Sequence of sections

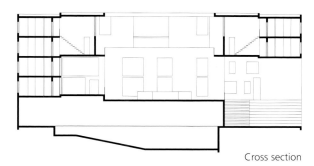

Cross section

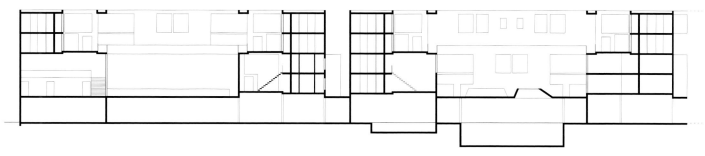

Longitudinal section

2nd upper floor

1st upper floor

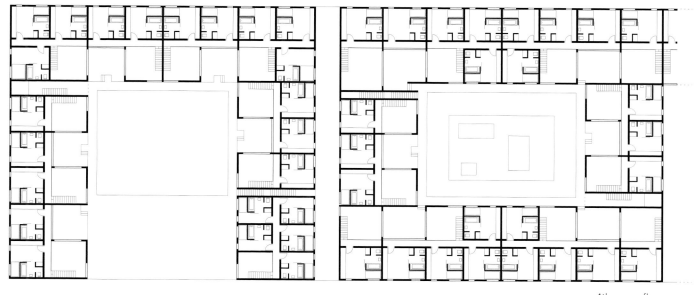

4th upper floor

3rd upper floor

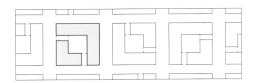

Perimeter block – perforated
Six storeys
All directions

The meandering form of the volume of the building is connected via three bridge-like elements that serve as circulation. The courtyards that result between them allow each section of the building to receive equal lighting. The two-storey spaces that puncture the building at intervals function as winter gardens and help provide daylight for the individual communal apartments. These spaces serve as a joint-access courtyard and can also be used to link neighbouring apartments.

The adjoining spaces are divided into a living and dining area and more private personal spaces, which with their own bathrooms serve as minimal self-contained private apartments. Combinations are possible by linking together different modules on either side of the winter gardens. Communal living areas and personal spaces can be combined in different ratios – either 1+5 or 3+3 – with different-sized winter gardens, either as single-storey or as two-storey gallery spaces. Accordingly, the configuration can vary from storey to storey, providing that they receive sufficient daylight.

Student project
Darmstadt University
Valeska Bühler

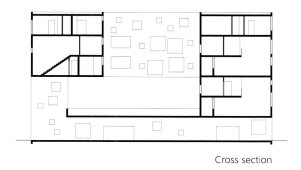

Cross section

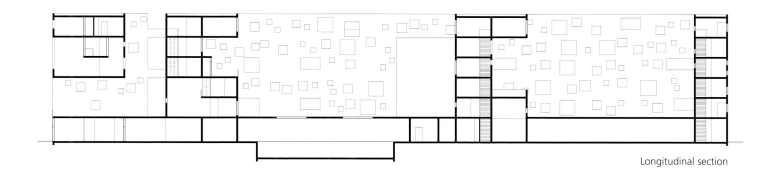

Longitudinal section

1st upper floor

3rd upper floor

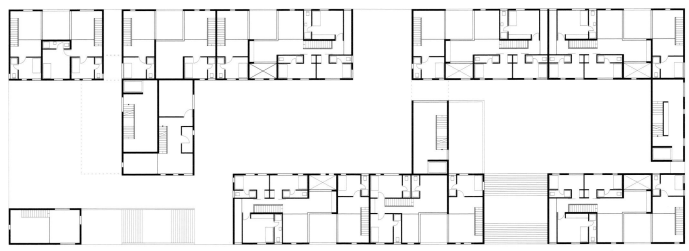

2nd upper floor

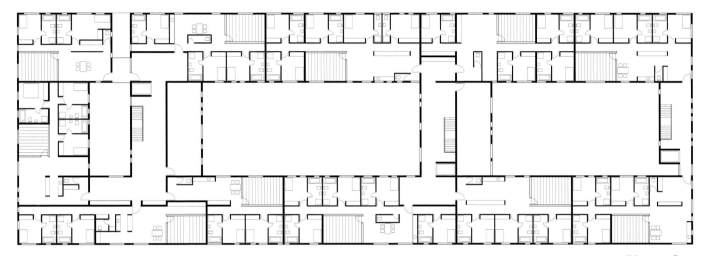

5th upper floor

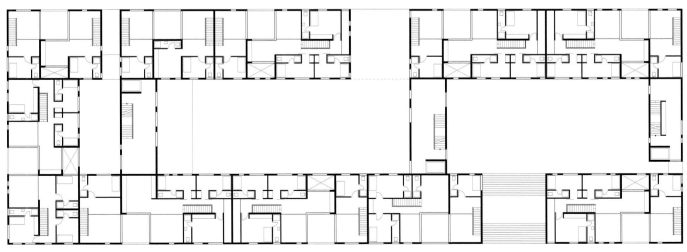

4th upper floor

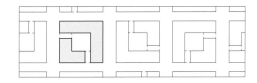

Perimeter block – perforated
Eight to nine storeys
All directions

Above a two-storey plinth for shops and commercial premises is a raised open platform reached by a broad flight of stairs. At regular intervals, stairwells with lifts connect the platform with the shopping arcades and underground parking in the floors below.

Each of the housing strips, whether arranged in an east-west direction or north-south direction, are systematically divided down the centre. Large loggias punctuate the otherwise rigorous arrangement. The system can accommodate both single-storey flats as well as larger maisonette apartments. The maisonettes are organised in such a way that the living areas switch from one side to the other for the floor above to benefit from daylight from both sides. As the concept employs a system with two or three flats per landing, the ability to combine flats with one another is only sometimes possible.

Student project
ETH Zurich
Philipp Zindel

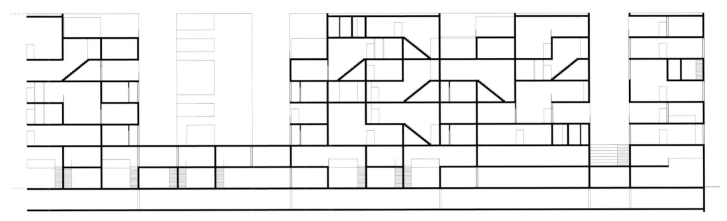

Longitudinal section

3rd upper floor

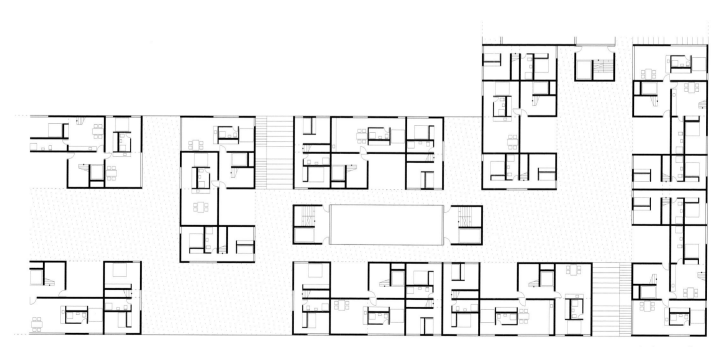

2nd upper floor

5th upper floor

4th upper floor

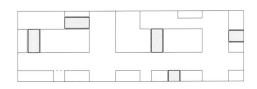

Infill
Four storeys
East-west orientation

The main characteristic of this infill project is its arrangement of individual "living boxes", which are stacked and combined to a height of four storeys. Six individual houses are interlocked in such a way that the upper-storey apartments can also be combined with one another in different constellations. The ground level zones contain additional small one and two-room apartments, though their illumination would not be sufficient for European standards. Access is via a series of passageways and irregularly arranged terraces in the interior of the block. The exceptionally small room sizes, together with the galleries and additional terraces, create a bustling feeling of houses within houses. The rooms and terraces on the upper storeys are well illuminated thanks to their east-west orientation.

Space Block Hanoi model
Hanoi, 2003
C+A Coelacanth and Associates

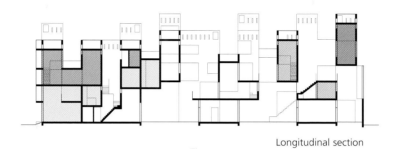

Longitudinal section

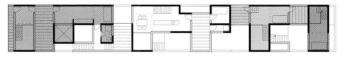

3rd upper floor

2nd upper floor

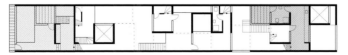

1st upper floor

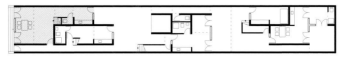

Ground floor

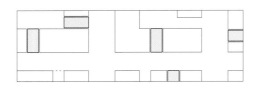

Infill
Five storeys
East-west orientation

At first glance, the building inserted into the vacant lot employs a straightforward rear-stair access typology. On closer inspection, the design affords a level of flexibility that all apartment housing should provide: it offers a variety of ways for the residents to adapt and personalise the rooms and sequence of rooms according to their own lifestyle. In addition to the stairwell with lift, a vertical riser for the installations has been located in such a way that a different living arrangement is possible on each floor, ranging from a fully open plan to a three-room apartment. On the third floor, the system accommodates a pair of two-room apartments, in the roof a large maisonette apartment with a second entrance from the staircase (as stipulated by Berlin's building regulations, but which also provides the added benefit of being able to separate the flat into two smaller units).

The fully-glazed façade with sliding aluminium screens likewise gives the residents free reign over how they wish to use and express the interior.

"Urbane Living 1"
Berlin, 2001
abcarius + burns architecture design

Cross section

Longitudinal section

2nd upper floor

Top floor

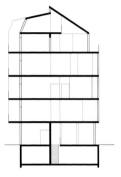

1st upper floor

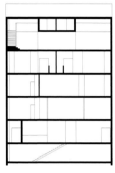

4th upper floor

Ground floor

3rd upper floor

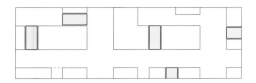

Infill
Five storeys
East-west orientation

This building, which fills a vacant site in a block perimeter in Berlin, consists of two interconnected houses. On the ground floor, both houses have a front and a rear entrance. The front entrance can also be used to access both units. A two-storey unit at the west end of the site contains a single private area and is connected via an elevated interior court on the first floor with the six-storey tower-like building to the east. This connection, as well as the connection on the ground floor, is optional, allowing the two units to be used together or separately as required at any time. The unit on the east is a single large dwelling with three private rooms and generous living areas on the second and fourth floors. While the smaller unit has a garden to the west, protected from view by a high wall, the living area of the larger unit is supplemented by a private terrace on the second floor and on the roof. A lift in the east part provides easier access to the tower.

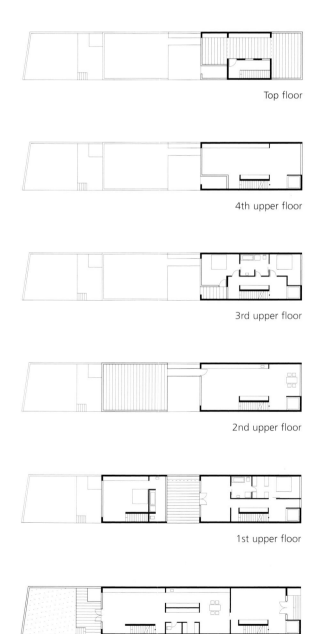

Top floor

4th upper floor

3rd upper floor

2nd upper floor

1st upper floor

Ground floor

Kunert town house
Berlin, 2006
Nalbach + Nalbach

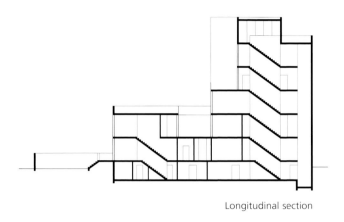

Longitudinal section

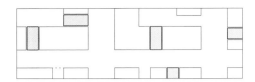

Infill
Five storeys
East-west orientation

This five-storey infill development cleverly combines commercial and private uses. Galleries and light wells next to the stairs in the commercial premises are skilfully used to interconnect the spaces, lending them interest and ensuring that they are well-lit. The residential function begins on the second floor with the main living room. The kitchen, dining area and living room are linked by a spacious roof terrace. To ensure that the upper floors are well-illuminated, the building depth of the upper storeys is reduced. The floors above the living room contain three private areas, each with their own naturally-lit bathroom and outdoor areas in the form of balconies. An additional terrace on the roof is linked with the uppermost floor. An ingenious arrangement of two stairs and a lift allows the residents to access the cellar separately, without having to cross paths with the commercial area.

Tilla Lindig Straub town house
Berlin, 2006
Nalbach + Nalbach

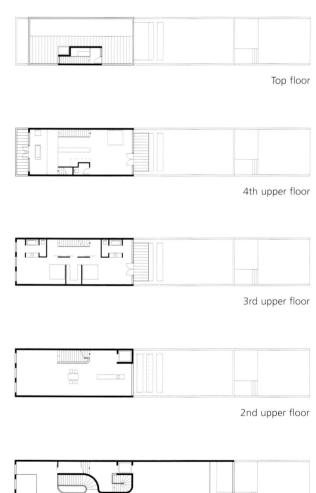

Top floor

4th upper floor

3rd upper floor

2nd upper floor

1st upper floor

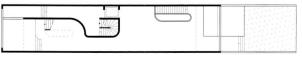

Ground floor

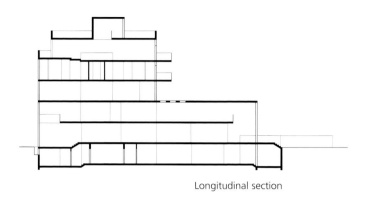

Longitudinal section

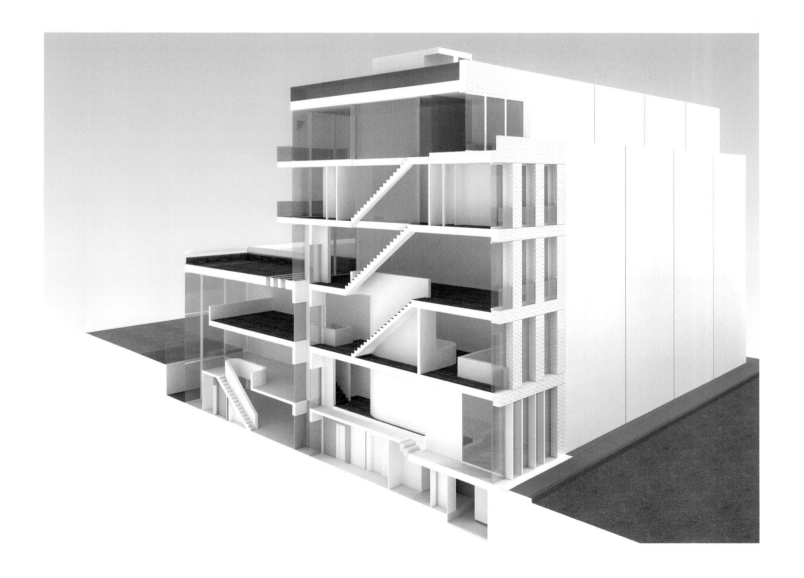

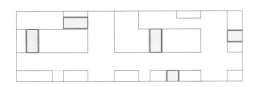

Infill
Six storeys
East-west orientation

Access to the loft house is via a compact interior core containing a dog-leg stair in the centre of the plan. The lift opens directly into each apartment. A walk-through sanitary strip with bathroom and optional separate toilet is arranged directly alongside the staircase. A free-standing vertical riser in the middle of the plan divides the open space into a kitchen, dining and living area. These simple structures offer the maximum possibility for personal adaptation and organisation of the apartment. The division of the living space is only dependent on the size and type of the kitchen and dining area.

The private rooms are divided by an optional walk-in closet allowing the rooms to be different sizes. Both of the one-room apartments at the entrance level, accessed from a central corridor, follow the same principle.

The subtle play of the fully-glazed bays on the east side and different-sized balconies is the only outward indication of the flexibility of the building within.

Loft house
Basel, 2002
Buchner Bründler AG

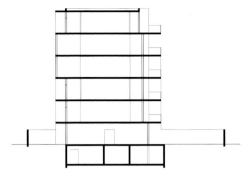

Longitudinal section

2nd upper floor

5th upper floor

1st upper floor

4th upper floor

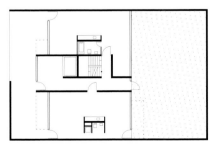

Ground floor

3rd upper floor

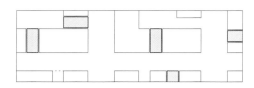

Infill
Seven storeys
East-west orientation

The entire depth of the site is utilised by using a bipartite arrangement of two buildings. A single-storey section is arranged along the entire length of the firewall on the south side, becoming two storeys as the topography of the site falls away. It contains apartments with split-level access which receive daylight via patios. The apartments vary in size according to their location in the building. Stairs from the terrace area and lifts within the building provide access to the upper floors. On the street side, the building fills the entire height of the infill site and is divided into two blocks connected by terraces slung between them that extend back deep into the site. Designed as outdoor areas for the flats, facing either east or west, these can also serve as open communal spaces for the residents. Due to draughty conditions, they remain largely unused. While the terraces help to reduce the volume of the building, the potential they offer for better illumination has not been exploited.

26 housing units
Paris, 1994
Philippe Gazeau

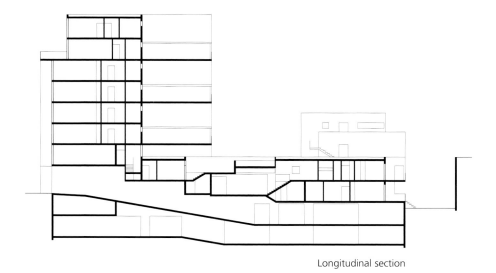

Longitudinal section

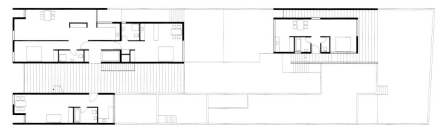

3rd upper floor

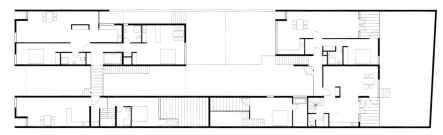

1st upper floor

Ground floor

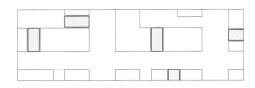

Infill
Eight storeys
East-west orientation

The two interlocking volumes of this building adjoin the firewalls of its neighbours but not along the full depth of the site. By offsetting the arrangement of both volumes on the 10.5-metre-wide site, the length of the frontage available to illuminate the apartments is more than doubled.

The staircase is arranged in the centre of the plan and provides access to a pair of spacious two-room apartments per floor. The structural difficulties of achieving the simple plans are skilfully concealed. At the end of the living areas with the glazed corner, there is a raised podium which is used as a seating bay. This conceals the bottom flange of a full-height Vierendeel truss which supports the cantilevered floor slabs and obviates the need for columns in the floor plan.

Fire regulations did not permit the provision of balconies. Instead a narrow projecting "runway" in front of the indented section of the façade creates a necessary visual boundary to the neighbour. Consistent with the column-free structure, all façades are fully glazed.

Lychener Straße housing
Berlin, 2001
Walter Nägeli and Sascha Zander

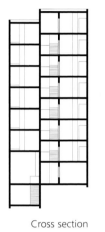

Cross section

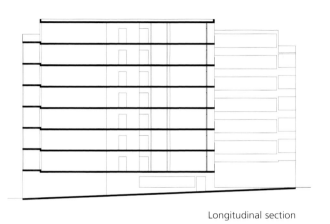

Longitudinal section

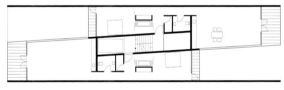

Top floor

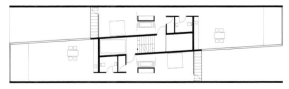

Typical floor plan

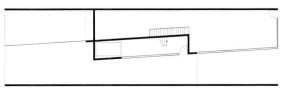

Ground floor

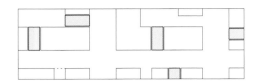

Infill
Five storeys
East-west orientation

The meandering form of this infill project is ideally suited for deep sites in the city – especially sites that span between two streets on either side of a block. The narrow building sections along the firewall are accessed from the north and have loggias facing south. These are the variable elements in the arrangement of the four buildings. The outer pair of buildings have lift access, the two buildings in the interior of the site are reached via an access deck on the first floor. All four buildings contain maisonette apartments stacked above one another. Accordingly, all rooms in the apartments are open across their entire depth from east to west; in addition, each apartment has a south-facing loggia. This principle can be applied in manifold permutations and the dimensions of the building sections and apartments can be varied. The permeability of the block can be achieved through the functions at ground level and via the deck on the first floor.

Student project
Darmstadt University
Martin Trefon

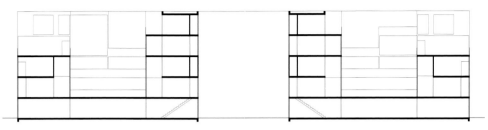

Longitudinal section

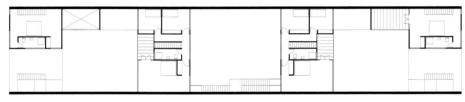

4th upper floor

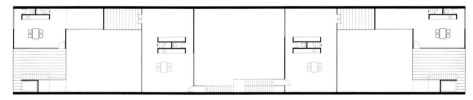

3rd upper floor

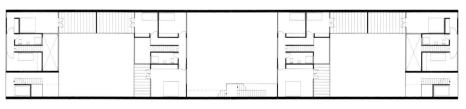

2nd upper floor

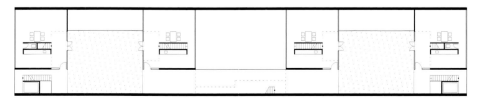

1st upper floor

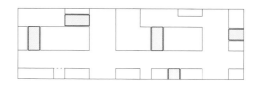

Infill
Five storeys
East-west orientation

This building type is designed for deep vacant sites that arise sporadically in the dense urban context of the city, often spanning between two parallel streets. Four semi-detached houses of differing types are arranged behind one another to achieve an appropriate urban density while maintaining sufficient distance from one another to ensure good illumination. This, together with outdoor spaces in the form of large terraces, contributes considerably to the quality of life in urban contexts.

The building in the middle is a back-to-back house type which is arranged so that the apartments switch sides on the second floor to avoid the disadvantages associated with single-aspect east or west-facing flats. A long single flight of stairs to the fourth floor provides access to the two-room roof apartment. Both of the outer buildings have a split-level arrangement. The back-to-back arrangement maximises the size of the court-yards between the buildings benefitting both house types.

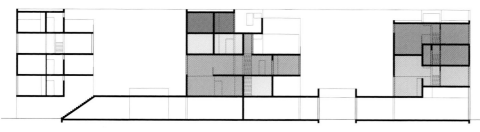

Longitudinal section

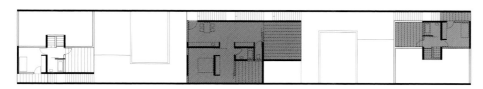

4th upper floor

3rd upper floor

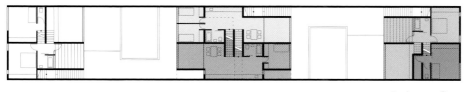

2nd upper floor

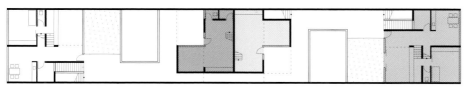

1st upper floor

Student project
Darmstadt University
Sebastian Schaal

125

Bibliography

Atelier 5: *Siedlungen und städtebauliche Projekte*. With an essay by Kenneth Frampton. Wiesbaden: Vieweg 1994

Asensio, Paco: *Wohnkonzepte für die Zukunft. Neue Konzepte für das klassische Einfamilienhaus*. Munich: Callwey 2003

Curtis, William J. R.: *Le Corbusier – Ideas and Forms*. New York: Rizzoli 1986

Durban, Christoph; Koch, Michael et al.: *Mehr als Wohnen. Gemeinnütziger Wohnungsbau in Zürich 1907-2007*. Zurich: gta 2007

Evans, Robin: "Figures, Doors and Passages", in: *Translations from Drawings to Building and other Essays*. London: AA Publications 1997, p. 55-91

Flagge, Ingeborg (Ed.): *Geschichte des Wohnens*. Vol. 1-5, 2nd edition; Ludwigsburg: Wüstenrot Foundation/Munich: DVA 1999

Gast, Klaus-Peter: *Living Plans. New Plans for Advanced Housing*. Basel, Boston, Berlin: Birkhäuser 2005

Gausa, Manuel: *Housing. New Alternatives, New Systems*. Basel, Boston, Berlin: Birkhäuser/Barcelona: Actar 1998

Geist, Jonas Friedrich; Kürvers, Klaus: *Das Berliner Mietshaus*. 3 volumes. Munich: Prestel 1980, 1988, 1993

Harlander, Tilman (Ed.): *Stadtwohnen. Geschichte, Städtebau, Perspektiven*. Ludwigsburg: Wüstenrot Foundation 2007

Hertzberger, Hermann: *Lessons for Students in Architecture*. 3rd updated edition; Rotterdam: 010 Publishers 1998

Komossa, Susanne; Meyer, Han et al.: *Atlas of the Dutch Urban Block*. Bussum: Thoth 2005

Koolhaas, Rem: "The Generic City", in: *S, M, L, XL*. New York: Monacelli Press 1995

Kruft, Hanno-Walther: *Geschichte der Architekturtheorie*. Munich: Verlag C. H. Beck 1991

Maretto, Paolo: *La casa veneziana nella storia della città, dall'origine all'Ottocento*. 4th edition; Venice: Marsilio Editori 1992

Rowe, Colin and Robert Slutzky: *Transparency*. 3rd updated edition; Basel, Boston, Berlin: Birkhäuser 1989

Schittich, Christian (Ed.): *In Detail. High-Density Housing: Concepts, Planning, Construction*. Basel, Boston, Berlin: Birkhäuser 2004

Schittich, Christian (Ed.): *In Detail. Housing for People of All Ages: flexible, unrestricted, senior-friendly*. Basel, Boston, Berlin: Birkhäuser 2007

Vetter, Andreas K.: *Townhouses*. Munich: Callwey 2008

Wüstenrot Foundation (Ed.): *Wohnbauen in Deutschland*. Stuttgart, Zurich: Krämer 2002

Wüstenrot Foundation, Deutscher Eigenheimverein e.V.: *Integriertes Wohnen im städtebaulichen Kontext*. Stuttgart, Zurich: Krämer 1998

Zophoniason-Baierl, Ulrike (Ed.): *Michael Alder. Das Haus als Typ*. Basel, Boston, Berlin: Birkhäuser 2006

Illustration credits

Philippe Gazeau
8, 96, 120
Andrea Kroth
13
Julie Peng, VG Bild-Kunst
19
Tomio Ohashi
21, 110
Floris Besserer
22
Michael Reisch
26
Michael Fontana
28
Wiel Arets Architects
30
Günter Pfeifer
32, 60, 92, 122
Alexander Gempeler
34, 35
Andrea Melbling
36, 37, 44, 47
Darlington Meier Architekten
40
Ruedi Walti
42, 118
Akiko + Hiroshi Takahashi workstation
48
Alexander Scholtysek
50
Darmstadt University
54, 56, 66, 84, 86, 98, 102
Atelier 5
62
Robertino Nikolic/arturimages
64
Francis Soler
70
Kathrin Hinkel
72

Martin Trefon
74
Oski Collado
78
C. F. Møller Architects
80
Herman Hertzberger
90 (above)
Jens Willebrand
90 (below)
Steven Holl Architects
94
Philipp Zindel
106, 107
Åke E:son Lindman
112
Nalbach + Nalbach
115, 117